Mustang

This book provides a critically informed account of the Turkey-born France-based director Deniz Gamze Ergüven's debut film *Mustang* (2015), which tells the story of five orphaned sisters living with their grandmother and uncle in a remote Turkish village.

The film's familiar art-house style, and its universalising focus on female coming-of-age and feminist dissent, resulted in celebratory reviews from journalists and scholars of world cinema. Meanwhile, *Mustang*'s framing of youth in the Turkish national context, and its representation of gender, divided Turkish film critics and cultural theorists. These divisions led to a debate that questions the politics of transnational feminism by criticising the film's failure to capture the local intricacies of the politics of gender and youth. While this book aims to locate *Mustang* within the intersection of emerging female and youth narratives in the cinema of Turkey, it also provides a critical understanding of the differences in *Mustang*'s local and global reception. This focus on the geopolitics of representation informs the diverse criteria this study uses to evaluate Ergüven's stylistic choices.

Engaging with both Anglophone and Turkish literature in youth cinema and gender studies, the book makes an original contribution to current debates on national/transnational cinemas and gender/youth studies and is an accessible reference for graduate and undergraduate study of contemporary film.

Elif Akçalı is Associate Professor in Film and TV Studies at Kadir Has University, Turkey. Her research focuses on film aesthetics, videographic criticism, non-fiction film, and gender/sexuality studies.

Cüneyt Çakırlar is Associate Professor in Film and Visual Culture at Nottingham Trent University, UK. His research focuses on issues of gender and sexuality in film and contemporary arts.

Özlem Güçlü is Assistant Professor in Sociology at Mimar Sinan Fine Arts University, Turkey. Her research focuses on gender and sexuality in cinema, cinema in Turkey, and cinematic animals.

Cinema and Youth Cultures

Cinema and Youth Cultures engages with well-known youth films from American cinema as well as the cinemas of other countries. Using a variety of methodological and critical approaches the series volumes provide informed accounts of how young people have been represented in film, while also exploring the ways in which young people engage with films made for and about them. In doing this, the Cinema and Youth Cultures series contributes to important and long-standing debates about youth cultures, how these are mobilized and articulated in influential film texts and the impact that these texts have had on popular culture at large.

Series Editors: Siân Lincoln and Yannis Tzioumakis

The Motorcycle Diaries
Youth, Travel and Politics in Latin America
Nadia Lie

Lady Bird
Self-Determination for a New Century
Rob Stone

Mustang
Translating Willful Youth
Elif Akçalı, Cüneyt Çakırlar, and Özlem Güçlü

Mary Poppins
Radical Elevation in the 1960s
Leslie H. Abramson

For more information about this series, please visit: www.routledge.com/Cinema-and-Youth-Cultures/book-series/CYC

Mustang
Translating Willful Youth

Elif Akçalı, Cüneyt Çakırlar, and Özlem Güçlü

LONDON AND NEW YORK

First published 2023
by Routledge
4 Park Square, Milton Park, Abingdon, Oxon OX14 4RN

and by Routledge
605 Third Avenue, New York, NY 10158

Routledge is an imprint of the Taylor & Francis Group, an informa business

© 2023 Elif Akçalı, Cüneyt Çakırlar and Özlem Güçlü

The right of Elif Akçalı, Cüneyt Çakırlar and Özlem Güçlü to be identified as authors of this work has been asserted in accordance with sections 77 and 78 of the Copyright, Designs and Patents Act 1988.

All rights reserved. No part of this book may be reprinted or reproduced or utilised in any form or by any electronic, mechanical, or other means, now known or hereafter invented, including photocopying and recording, or in any information storage or retrieval system, without permission in writing from the publishers.

Trademark notice: Product or corporate names may be trademarks or registered trademarks, and are used only for identification and explanation without intent to infringe.

British Library Cataloguing-in-Publication Data
A catalogue record for this book is available from the British Library

ISBN: 978-0-367-54313-6 (hbk)
ISBN: 978-0-367-54384-6 (pbk)
ISBN: 978-1-003-08905-6 (ebk)

DOI: 10.4324/9781003089056

Typeset in Times New Roman
by Newgen Publishing UK

Contents

List of Figures vi
Series Editors' Introduction vii
Acknowledgements ix

Introduction: Locating *Mustang's* Willful Youth 1

1 Escaping New Turkey's 'Wife Factory': Towards a Contextualisation of the Claim for Female Voice and Subjectivity 22

2 Framing the Willful Subject of Coming-of-Age: Cinematography and Stylistic Excess 42

3 Critical Reception: Paradoxes of National Belonging and Geopolitics of Film Criticism 67

Conclusions 92

References 98
Index 109

Figures

0.1	Child Stars of Turkish Cinema: Ayşecik (top left) in *Ayşecikle Ömercik* (1969), Sezercik (top right) in *Sezercik Aslan Parçası* (1972), Emrah (bottom left) in *Ayrılamam* (1986), Ceylan (bottom right) in *Yuvasızlar* (1987)	5
0.2	Handan and Behiye in *2 Genç Kız / 2 Girls* (2005)	8
0.3	Hayat, her father, and her grandfather in *Hayat Var / My Only Sunshine* (2008)	8
1.1	The sisters' play at the beach with their classmates in *Mustang*	24
1.2	Teacher's embrace at the final scene in *Mustang*	39
2.1	*Mustang*'s five-headed 'Monster Femininity'	45
2.2	Spaces of flight in *Mustang*	55
2.3	Windows as melodramatic trope in *Mustang*	56
2.4	House as cage in *Mustang*	57
2.5	Grandmother's house in *Mustang*	60
2.6	Delacroix's *Liberty* in *Mustang*	60
2.7	The maternal closet and the Gezi t-shirt in *Mustang*	61
2.8	The politics of pink and red in *Mustang*	64
2.9	'Shit-coloured' dresses in *Mustang*	65

Series Editors' Introduction

Despite the high visibility of youth films in the global media marketplace – especially since the 1980s when Conglomerate Hollywood realised that such films were not only strong box office performers but also the starting point for ancillary sales in other media markets, as well as for franchise building – academic studies that focused specifically on such films were slow to materialise. Arguably the most important factor behind academia's reluctance to engage with youth films was a (then) widespread perception within the Film and Media Studies communities that such films held little cultural value and significance, and therefore were not worthy of serious scholarly research and examination. Just like the young subjects they represented, whose interests and cultural practices have been routinely deemed transitional and transitory, so were the films that represented them perceived as fleeting and easily digestible, destined to be forgotten quickly, as soon as the next youth film arrived on cinema screens a week later.

Under these circumstances, and despite a small number of pioneering studies in the 1980s and early 1990s, the field of 'youth film studies' did not really start blossoming and attracting significant scholarly attention until the 2000s and in combination with similar developments in cognate areas such as 'girl studies'. However, because of the paucity of material in the previous decades, the majority of these new studies in the 2000s focused primarily on charting the field, and therefore steered clear of long, in-depth examinations of youth films, or were exemplified by edited collections that chose particular films to highlight certain issues to the detriment of others. In other words, despite providing often wonderfully rich accounts of youth cultures as these have been captured by key films, these studies could not have possibly dedicated sufficient space to engage with more than just a few key aspects of youth films.

In more recent years (post-2010) a number of academic studies started delimiting their focus and therefore providing more space for in-depth examinations of key types of youth films, such as slasher films and biker films or examining youth films in particular historical periods. From that point on, it was only a matter of time for the first publications that focused exclusively on key youth films from a number of perspectives to appear (*Mamma Mia! The Movie*, *Twilight* and *Dirty Dancing* are among the first films to receive this treatment). Conceived primarily as edited collections, these studies provided a multifaceted analysis of these films, focusing on such issues as: the politics of representing youth; the stylistic and narrative choices that characterise these films and the extent to which they are representative of a youth cinema; the ways these films address their audiences; the ways youth audiences engage with these films; the films' industrial location and other relevant issues.

It is within this increasingly maturing and expanding academic environment that the **Cinema and Youth Cultures** volumes arrive, aiming to consolidate existing knowledge, provide new perspectives, apply innovative methodological approaches, offer sustained and in-depth analyses of key films and therefore become the 'go to' resource for students and scholars interested in theoretically informed, authoritative accounts of youth cultures in film. As editors, we have tried to be as inclusive as possible in our selection of key examples of youth films by commissioning volumes on films that span the history of cinema, including the silent film era; that portray contemporary youth cultures as well as ones associated with particular historical periods; that represent examples of mainstream and independent cinema; that originate in American cinema and the cinemas of other nations; that attracted significant critical attention and commercial success during their initial release and that were 'rediscovered' after an unpromising initial critical reception. Together these volumes are going to advance youth film studies while also being able to offer extremely detailed examinations of films that are now considered significant contributions to cinema and our cultural life more broadly.

We hope readers will enjoy the series.

Siân Lincoln & Yannis Tzioumakis
Cinema & Youth Cultures Series Editors

Acknowledgements

This book is the result of a passionate friendship and a genuine collaborative effort. This unforgettable journey has shown us the immeasurably restorative value of collaboration and slow scholarship despite the atomising market forces of contemporary academia. We would like to thank Siân Lincoln, Martin O'Shaughnessy, and Yannis Tzioumakis for their encouragement.

There is no 'first author' in this book. Our names appear in alphabetical order and all parts of the book are co-authored with equal contributions from each author.

Introduction
Locating *Mustang*'s Willful Youth

This book aims to provide a critically informed account of the Turkey-born France-based director Deniz Gamze Ergüven's debut film *Mustang* (2015), which tells the story of five orphaned sisters living with their grandmother and uncle in a remote Turkish village. Narrating these five characters' rapport with the conservative and segregated gender order in which they are trained for and coerced into arranged marriages, this unconventional coming-of-age story capitalises upon solidarity, agency, and resistance rather than a defeatist drama of spectacular victimhood. The film's familiar art-house style, and its universalising focus on female coming-of-age and feminist dissent resulted in celebratory reviews from journalists and scholars of world cinema. Meanwhile, *Mustang*'s framing of youth in the Turkish national context, and its representation of gender, divided Turkish film critics and cultural theorists. These divisions resulted in a debate that questions the politics of transnational feminism by criticising the film's failure to capture the local intricacies of the politics of gender and youth. The book provides a critical understanding of the differences in *Mustang*'s local and global reception, especially as these pertain to the representation of youth femininities on screen and as this representation is informed by the diverse criteria used to evaluate Ergüven's stylistic choices and her engagement with the national context. Engaging with both Anglophone and Turkish literature in film and gender studies, the book makes a critical intervention into current debates on national/transnational cinemas and gender/youth studies.

As a productive example of interstitial filmmaking, *Mustang* bears significant potential to critically explore the categorical complexities of national, transnational, and migrant/diasporic cinemas. While it was made in Turkey, with a cast, characters, and story from Turkey, and filmed in the Turkish language, the context in which *Mustang* was funded, produced, and distributed throughout the world calls for a

DOI: 10.4324/9781003089056-1

2 *Introduction*

critical investigation of its affinities with Turkish and European cinemas. Furthermore, the subject of female coming-of-age and the film's stylistic excess offer a point of entry into the debates on women's filmmaking in world cinemas, and the geopolitics of its national and international reception. As neither the background nor the career of the film's director, Deniz Gamze Ergüven, sit harmoniously with the familiar brands of diasporic authorship and its 'accented' aesthetics, the affirmative feminism within *Mustang*'s representation of youth, and its polarised critical reception in Turkey, France, and the Anglophone circles of film criticism, call for an analytical framework that is shaped by a nuanced understanding of *transnationalism as method* in film studies.

Therefore, in this book, reading *Mustang* becomes a practice of revising conventional tendencies in viewing and interpreting a transnational film, as its global and local reception affix the film's interpretations into limited frameworks consolidated by preconceived ideas of how European or Turkish films are or should be. *Mustang*'s interstitial location within the conceptual frameworks of film studies allows the authors of the book to experiment with a critical literacy that contests the geopolitically constructed registers of transnational and national cinemas by treating the film's mobility (across national borders and categorical distinctions) through a non-identitarian framework.

Mustang can also be located within the global revival of youth and coming-of-age narratives in film and television cultures. While the proliferation of contemporary youth narratives could be framed as a global trend, our account of *Mustang*'s expressive style and its engagement with national politics will facilitate a debate that not only traces the potential influences global youth films have on particular contexts of national cinema but also rethinks how the local intricacies of Turkey's socio-political context are integrated into a film with obscure national belongings, and how its representation of youth is received nationally and internationally. Our aim is not to offer a universalising approach to transnational women's filmmaking, but to underline the complexity of factors that define a film's style, production, and reception, which are informed by conventions and expectations embedded within the networks of film industry and criticism. These conventions produce regimes of intelligibility through which a film becomes palatable to certain audiences. Indeed, such sectoral conditions of palatability in the film market are informed by the ways in which cultural practices appropriate, contest, and even obscure the contemporary political contexts and the paradigms of nationality these practices are situated in.

In their critical account of the 'proliferation of the term "transnational" as a potentially empty, floating signifier', Higbee and Lim call for a 'critical transnationalism [that] might help us interpret more productively the interface between local and global, national, and transnational, as well as moving away from a binary approach to national/transnational and from a Eurocentric tendency of how such films might be read' (2010: 10). A 'critical transnationalism', Higbee and Lim assert, 'does not ghettoise transnational film-making in interstitial and marginal spaces but rather interrogates how these film-making activities negotiate with the national on all levels – from cultural policy to financial sources, from the multiculturalism of difference to how it reconfigures the nation's image of itself' (18). We contend that studying *Mustang*, through its style, authorship, reception, and engagement with the national, could further nuance the ways in which critical transnationalism could be implemented as method in film studies. The subject of coming-of-age in *Mustang* is key to the book's analytical framework, as we argue that Ergüven's affirmative optic of willful youth determines the film's negotiation – and *dissonance* – with the national in terms of style, genre, representation, gender politics, and spectatorial address.

Absence/Presence of Willfulness

Until the early 2000s, the representations of childhood, youth, and coming-of-age in the cinema of Turkey had been used as narrative devices to project patriarchal constructions of family and citizenship. During the Yeşilçam period (covering the 1960s, the 1970s, and the 1980s), when film production in Turkey reached its peak, most of the films featuring child protagonists thematised adult anxieties stemming from complexities of love and marriage in a class-divided society. Especially in the 1960s, Yeşilçam sees a promotion of child protagonists such as Ayşecik, Sezercik, and Yumurcak who become famous in hit sequels (e.g. *Çöpçatan / The Matchmaker* [İnanoğlu 1962], *Ayşecik Canımın İçi / Ayşecik My Dearest* [Saner 1963], *Ayşecik Cimcime Hanım / Ayşecik Naughty Lady* [Saner 1964], *Ayşecik Sokak Kızı / Ayşecik Street Girl* [Erakalın 1966], *Yumurcak* [İnanoğlu 1969], *Yumurcak Köprü Altı Çocuğu* [İnanoğlu 1970], *Sezercik Küçük Mücahit* [Göreç 1974], and *Yumurcak Belalı Tatil / The Man from Chicago* [Koloğlu, Melikyan, and Pallardy 1975]) (see Figure 0.1). However, even as heroes and heroines, the children and the youth in these early examples are not granted personal and critical voices against the traditional patriarchal values that are smoothly restored in the films' endings. Embodying an adult position of identification, these characters are used to produce a melodramatic pathos for adult spectators. Most of these characters are part of a household or are represented as orphans whose ultimate purpose is to belong to a family. Whether through comedy or melodrama – the two popular genres of Yeşilçam – these characters celebrate heterosexual love ripped off from its sexuality and they embody a promise of continuity of family. During the Yeşilçam era, we also see famous adult actors taking roles as teens, such as those in *Hababam Sınıfı / The Chaos Class* (Eğilmez 1975) and *Neşeli Günler / Happy Days* (Aksoy 1978). The agency of these subjects of youth and coming-of-age is collapsed into a hegemonic national will. In other words, neither the cute children nor the infantilised adults in these films are willful. We will shortly elaborate what we mean by 'will' and 'willfulness'.

The years leading to the military coup in 1980 are marked by civil unrest and violence in the Turkish public sphere, followed by a halt in cultural and artistic production including cinema. During the coup years, the rise of *arabesk* music had led to the production of the genre's own child-stars who become famous through films. While the characters they perform were child heroes, they were neither youthful nor childlike. They were the most popular symbols of coming-of-age in the 1980s although they do not signify willful youth. Emrah and Ceylan, the two most famous child stars of the *arabesk* era, are trapped in a young body, but are overwhelmed with adult anxieties, projecting the societal corruption of class and gender inequalities (e.g. *Zavallılar / The Poor Ones* [Efekan 1984], *Acıların Çocuğu / The Child of Pains* [Efekan 1985], *Boynu Bükükler* [Efekan 1985], *Öksüzler / Orphans* [Göreç 1986], *Beni Bende Bitirdiler* [Saydam 1989], and *Hep Ezildim* [Gürsu 1989]) (see Figure 0.1). While they resemble Yeşilçam's child stars in terms of their ventriloquising the 'general will' of patriarchal familialism, these orphaned children of *arabesk* cinema were 'browner, prouder, and poorer' which demonstrated class inequalities and stratification following the Kurdish migration to the bigger Turkish cities (Pamak 2019; Gürbilek 2001). In her commentary on the affective currency of the image of Giovanni Brogalin's *The Crying Boy*, which widely circulated in Turkish popular culture, Gürbilek suggests that such an investment in the sorrowful image of a white Western child mirrors not only Yeşilçam's popular child stars as embodiments of Turkish republican idealism but also the denial of Turkey's 'brown, provincial children' and their sorrow (ibid.: 43). While *arabesk* films of the 1980s manage to deviate from Yeşilçam's idealised orphans by integrating a different social reality (informed by the provinces i.e. *taşra*) into their narratives of childhood and coming-of-age, these characters' agency or willfulness remains absent (or markedly aligned with the general will). This paradoxical visibility of youth in Turkish cinema during the Yeşilçam era and the *arabesk* films of the 1980s shifts to a different

Introduction 5

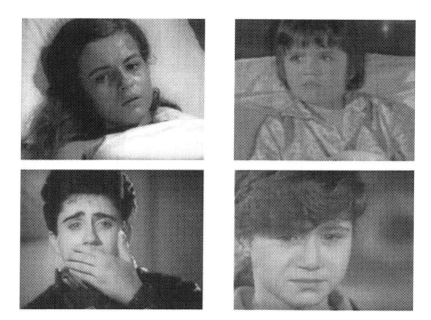

Figure 0.1 Child Stars of Turkish Cinema: Ayşecik (top left) in *Ayşecikle Ömercik* (1969), Sezercik (top right) in *Sezercik Aslan Parçası* (1972), Emrah (bottom left) in *Ayrılamam* (1986), Ceylan (bottom right) in *Yuvasızlar* (1987).

repertoire of willful youth in post-millennial Turkish filmmaking, following the invisibility of children in the cinema of the 1990s.

To account for *Mustang*'s representation of willful youth (and its critical reception), this historical trajectory of 'will' in cinema matters a great deal to the authors of the volume. In this sense, Sara Ahmed's conceptual framework in *Willful Subjects* (2014) makes a significant contribution to the analytical approach developed throughout this book. Ahmed's nuanced re-formulation of cultural resistance and dissidence through her rigorous re-conceptualisation of 'will' and 'willfulness' guides our core objective to locate *Mustang* within the theoretical paradigms of style, genre, authorship, context, reception, and politics of intelligibility. 'If authority assumes the right to turn a wish into a command', Ahmed suggests, 'then willfulness is a diagnosis of the failure to comply with those whose authority is given' (1). The willful subject, in Ahmed's study, is a subject that turns her 'particular will' away from the 'general will' while the hegemonic forces work to

6 *Introduction*

align them (173). Therefore, the subject of coming-of-age (or that of childhood and youth) becomes a fertile ground to trace the ways in which will and willfulness inform subjectivity. It is the gap which widens between the particular will and the general will, that the post-millennial youth films in Turkish cinema (as well as the global revival of coming-of-age films) have mobilised. In this regard, we argue that there is a significant shift in the history of Turkish cinema, from an absence of 'particular will' (as seen in Yeşilçam's representation of childhood and youth) to a remarkable proliferation of 'willful subjects' on screen. We contend that *Mustang*'s style and contextual engagement, informed by its interstitial authorship, deviate from the familiar aesthetic trends of post-millennial Turkish cinema and its representation of willful youth, which contributes to its polarised critical reception.

In post-millennial Turkish filmmaking, we recognise an increase in the figures of adolescents, youth, and young adults as main protagonists who are noticeably different than their earlier counterparts. The children and youth of classical Turkish cinema mostly served as narrative devices to prioritise heteronormative coupling and patriarchal family, and, therefore, write and reinforce social and cultural scripts of 'proper' adulthood, i.e. the 'right' path to follow. However, examples of post-millennial filmmaking in Turkey provide not only the types of youth that these scripts approve of, but also the ones that 'stray away' and contest these hegemonic scripts in various ways. Most of these young characters have personal and/or critical voices, a 'particular will' to use Sara Ahmed's terminology, against the 'parental will' or the 'general will', while asserting their own desires. They discover and explore their sexualities (e.g. *2 Genç Kız / 2 Girls* [Ataman 2005], *Hayat Var / My Only Sunshine* [Erdem 2008], *Mavi Dalga / The Blue Wave* [Dadak and Kayan 2013], *Zenne / The Dancer* [Alper and Binay 2011], *Bilmemek / Not Knowing* [Yılmaz 2019]); they question familial attachments (e.g. *Koca Dünya / Big Big World* [Erdem 2016], *Zenne*, *Hayat Var*); they despise norms of parenting (e.g. *Çoğunluk / Majority* [Yüce 2010]); they explore (un)belonging (e.g. *Kar / Snow* [Erdoğdu 2017], *Bornova Bornova* [Temelkuran 2009], *Çoğunluk*, *Arada / In Between* [Tunç 2018]); they feel anxious of their future (eg. *Arada*, *Başka Semtin Çocukları / Children of the Otherside* [Bulut 2008], *Kara Köpekler Havlarken / Black Dogs Barking* [Er and Gorbach 2009], *Çekmeköy Underground* [Türkmen 2014]); they resist against class inequalities (e.g. *Nefesim Kesilene Kadar / Until I Lose My Breath* [Balcı 2015], *Çekmeköy Underground*, *Şimdiki Zaman / Present Tense* [Söylemez 2012]); they contest ethnic discrimination (e.g. *Bahoz / Storm* [Öz 2008], *Annemin Şarkısı / My Mother's Song* [Mintaş 2014]) and gender-based violence (e.g. *2 Genç Kız*, *Hayat*

Var, Tereddüt / Clair-Obscur [Ustaoğlu 2016], *Sibel* [Zencirci and Giovanetti 2018], *Kızkardeşler / A Tale of Three Sisters* [Alper 2019]); and they confront silenced collective traumas of the national past (e.g. *Kaygı / Inflame* [Özçelik 2017], *Sonbahar / Autumn* [Alper 2008], *Gelecek Uzun Sürer / Future Lasts Forever* [Alper 2011], *Babamın Sesi / Voice of My Father* [Eskiköy 2015][1]). It is significant that this revival of youth films, dealing with various themes and subjects, coincides with Turkey's governing Justice and Development Party's (AKP) revised emphasis, both in public speeches and party policies, on raising a pious and moral youth. Moreover, most of these films, including *Mustang*, were released after the Gezi protests, where the vast majority of protestors who rose up against governmental authoritarianism and moralism endangering secular lifestyles were young (*Konda* 2014). Director Deniz Gamze Ergüven stated in several interviews (Arman 2015; Gürcü 2015a) that Gezi uprisings had inspired *Mustang*. Proliferation of these youth films in this specific timeframe can be considered as a cultural response to the AKP's political drive to 'bend' youth towards the dominant national will marked with patriarchal values of family and religious piety.

2 Genç Kız and *Hayat Var* mark the earliest significant examples of this proliferation. Sustaining a queer tension throughout its coming-of-age narrative, *2 Genç Kız* represents its two young female characters, Behiye and Handan, as misfits and wanderers who pursue their own will and desire with a youthful energy, disdaining ideals of 'proper' adulthood and contesting the general heteronormative family unit as toxic, violent, or dysfunctional (see Figure 0.2). Likewise, the coming-of-age story of Hayat in *Hayat Var* represents family as violent and suffocating (Çakırlar and Güçlü 2013). Recalling the *arabesk* motifs of the previous period, Hayat, in this film, bears the burdens of growing up as an adult-child, taking care of relatives and household chores.[2] However, her silent and willful presence, especially against family members and the rules of patriarchal gender order, calls 'general will' or 'parental will' into question[3] (see Figure 0.3). *Mustang*'s protagonists, the five sisters, bear traces of these willful characters. Behiye's rage, Handan's joy, and Hayat's apathy resonate with the sisters' different responses to what Sara Ahmed terms the 'rod' of patriarchal family as a 'straightening device' (2014: 7, 114), that is, straightening the straying/deviating will of the willful child, and defining 'proper' womanhood.

Mustang's critical response to the ideal of 'proper' womanhood also echoes the emergent genre of rom-coms in the contemporary cinema of Turkey, yet with a significant difference. After more than two decades of absence (and more than a decade after the 'chick-flick' flow in global cinema), the 'resurrection' of rom-coms in Turkish

8 *Introduction*

Figure 0.2 Handan and Behiye in *2 Genç Kız / 2 Girls* (2005).

Figure 0.3 Hayat, her father, and her grandfather in *Hayat Var / My Only Sunshine* (2008).

cinema in the 2010s (Güçlü 2017) appears as one remarkable trend. In contrast to the classical rom-com's focus on coupledom, these films revolve around their young female protagonists' 'desperate singleton' while prioritising female subjective points of view through distinctive uses of formal and stylistic elements, such as monologue, point of view shot, voice-over, flashback, and dream or fantasy sequences (192). With titles like *Kocan Kadar Konuş / Husband Factor* (Baruönü 2015), *Kocan Kadar Konuş: Diriliş / Husband Factor: Resurrection* (Baruönü 2016), *Romantik Komedi / Romantic Comedy* (Ketche 2010), *Romantik Komedi: Bekarlığa Veda / Romantic Comedy: Stag Party* (Özlevi 2013), *Hadi İnşallah / Hopefully* (Baltacı 2014), these new rom-coms criticise the obsession with marriage, traditional gender roles, and hegemonic 'ideals' of femininity. The critical potential of this emerging trend is particularly notable as Turkish cinema has worked for so long like a 'wife-factory' – recalling the youngest sister Lale's words in *Mustang* – that 'straightened' its young characters' agency in aligning it with the general will, glorifying heterosexual marriage, and confining women's roles in the 'sacred' family union. Despite this critical potential, young willful women characters of these new rom-coms forfeit their personal will and agency for romance and marriage. Their willfulness is ultimately tamed with the pursuit of a 'true' romance and a husband when the stories find closure (Güçlü 2017: 204–6).

Even though some of these young protagonists smoothly bend towards the general will at the end of films (like these new rom-coms) and the main focus may not be the willfulness of the main characters, an increasing number of films that revolve around willful young female protagonists appear in contemporary Turkish cinema. From the point of view of the willful youth, these films bring into focus the capacity for and possibility of saying or enacting a 'no' (Ahmed 2014: 55) to what they are expected to do by cultural and social scripts of 'proper' adulthood/womanhood. Yet, *Mustang* stands out among these films as an epitome of the tension between the general will and the particular will as the film's subject matter is the sisters' willful positions – how each girl willfully negotiates (un)becoming, something that defines the phase of coming-of-age. There are also important examples of male coming-of-age and youth dramas that uncover this tension by problematising the patriarchal family unit (e.g. *Çoğunluk*, *Sivas* [Müjdeci 2014], *Üç Maymun / Three Monkeys* [Ceylan 2008], *Ahlat Ağacı / Wild Pear Three* [Ceylan 2018]). However, they do not openly deal with the tension between the two wills.

Furthermore, even though the other examples may not directly problematise this tension, and their narratives may be based on alternative storylines and (un)dramatic events – sometimes with no tension or conflict (e.g. *Mavi Dalga, Şimdiki Zaman*) – it is important to note that they offer unfitting, indifferent, lost, rebellious, confused characters who, even sometimes momentarily, signal a possibility to hold/arrest the narrative against the expected course of events. This is a possibility to divert, relapse, resume, be in-between, stay still, not go straight, not go as slow or as fast, not go at all. Sara Ahmed argues:

> Normalcy can be understood in terms of function: having a part that can do, and is willing to do, what it is assumed for ('willing and able'). Being willing might be required when one is not able ('willing not able'). Compulsory able-bodiedness could be thought of as a will duty as well as a productive duty: a body that is not whole, that has non-functioning parts, must be willing if not able, or willing to be able.
>
> (Ahmed 2014: 109–10)

Contemporary examples from Turkey may not take willfulness as their central subject matter – as *Mustang* does – but they contain characters that may be deemed as unconventional or dysfunctional in classical cinematic storytelling: these characters are killjoys, drifters, misfits. They occupy the filmic space and *mise-en-scène* in terms of shot duration or shot size as much as they arrest the narratives hanging in time and space. The resistance against the general will (be it parental, national, etc.) in the story is reflected in how they are framed or how these willful characters occupy the narrative continuity. Therefore, these films offer the viewer a frame to see the weight, burden, or inertia of youth as an effect of coming-of-age.

This effect is very much visible throughout the whole narrative in *Mustang* as it directly revolves around the tension between the general will and the personal will; the young sisters' (un)becoming 'proper' women at the risk of their lives. However, this weight or burden is uniquely merged by claiming joy and hope for the protagonists as willful women. In this respect, *Sibel* seems like the closest 'sister' film to *Mustang*, as it is an important example that problematises a similar tension through its young female character, who stands like what Sara Ahmed considers as a 'raised arm' (2014: 194–7) against the expectations of a patriarchal village life. However, *Sibel*'s almost dystopic atmosphere does not break until the very end, where the young protagonist takes her sister's side against the whole village's shaming, and exchanges a smile with a young village girl. At that moment, the characteristic slow pace of the film also breaks down and gives way to a rap song's fast rhythm. Only in this very moment does *Sibel* catch *Mustang*'s unique youthful and hopeful energy resisting victimisation. Together with its embrace of over-exposed willfulness of female youth, *Mustang*'s most significant difference among other youth films lies exactly at this point. While many of these films bring forward the hopeless and futureless worlds of their young characters (Liktor 2021), *Mustang* claims hope for its youngest sisters, both with its ending and through its narrative and stylistic choices. Such a claim becomes also remarkable if one considers the AKP's contemporary gender politics against which the film takes a clear stand. While women and the young are the two main realms through which the governing party has aimed to sustain authoritarian social control in Turkey for years, *Mustang* directly responds to this gender regime of familialism and anti-feminism with a hopeful claim for female youth. Today, this political context reached a grim milestone when Turkey scandalously withdrew from the İstanbul Convention (Council of Europe Convention on Preventing and Combating Violence Against Women and Domestic Violence). In this context – in which male violence against women perpetuates impunity, the hate speech against LGBTQ+ people comes from representatives of state institutions, and hate crimes against the member of these communities increasingly continue – *Mustang*'s own willfulness, its enactment of a 'no' to this hateful and violent gender regime, with a claim of hope for female youth, deserves close attention.

Global Trends of Coming-of-Age Film

Because of its interstitial nature, *Mustang* needs to be positioned and discussed amongst a broad number and range of contemporary global youth films. There is an apparent rise of youth narratives on screens, ranging from art-house films that meet audiences primarily through festivals (e.g. *Blue is the Warmest Colour* [Kechiche 2013], *Girlhood* [Sciamma 2014], *American Honey* [Arnold 2016], and *Burning* [Changdong 2018]) to popular series that are distributed worldwide via streaming platforms (e.g. *Sex Education* [Netflix 2019–], *Euphoria* [HBO 2019–], *I May Destroy You* [BBC & HBO 2020], and *Heartstopper* [Netflix 2022]). Youth-centred narratives have common thematic strands that have been historically shaped around anxieties of growing up, resistance and rebellion against institutional norms and conformism, and hopes and delusions attached to youthful energy and desire. These films have been categorised as teen, adolescent, youth, and/or coming-of-age films in various academic studies (Shary 2004; Shary and Seibel 2007; Berghahn 2009; Berghahn and Sternberg 2010; Driscoll 2011; Colling

12 *Introduction*

2017; Smith 2017; Chareyron and Viennot 2019) to reduce and negotiate the complexities of heterogeneity in style and narration across different modes and cultures of film production.

The association of certain generic conventions of popular cinema adopted from mainstream Hollywood with the category of teen film inhibits us from utilising this term in our discussion. *Mustang* does not belong to the teen genre, neither as a global nor a local example. Even though it deals with teen film's narrative conventions as outlined by Driscoll, such as 'the youthfulness of central characters; [...] intense age-based peer relationships and conflict either within those relationships or with an older generation; the institutional management of adolescence by families, schools and other institutions; and coming-of-age plots focused on motifs like virginity, graduation, and the makeover' (2011: 2), stylistically it neither adopts the global mainstream Anglophone aesthetics of teen film nor the contemporary popular comedy and romance films involving youth narratives in Turkey. Moreover, the film is not marketed specifically for an adolescent audience, which marks another criterion for the genre (Shary 2004; Colling 2017). Therefore, labelling *Mustang* as such would complicate our discussions around style and context. The distinction that Driscoll makes between 'youth' and 'teen' film in her earlier study *Girls* (2002) – which she later disputes (2011: 3) – is useful for our book, especially because she attaches rebellion to the former and commodity culture to the latter. She writes, 'teen and youth film genres have interacted with each other and helped cast into public culture a distinction between rebellious youth and difficult teen life [...] This distinction claims that youth subcultures are eternally rebellious, whereas the teenage world based around school and home is, unless exceptional and subcultural, mainstream and conformist' (2002: 218). Driscoll's discussion of youth narratives as pushing against the indefinite boundaries of what a young person should (not) be or do resonates well with our positioning of coming-of-age films through the reading of *Mustang*, which locates the subject of youth at the intersections between will and willfulness. Driscoll's use of youth as 'a liminal position' (206) also stresses the unsettled aspects of growing up. In fact, in her more recent work, Driscoll evokes the concept of liminality when writing about coming-of-age and rite-of-passage narratives, and defines adolescence as 'both transitional and a non-place' (Driscoll 2011: 112). Quoting Adrian Martin (1994; see also Martin 1989), Driscoll takes the liminal experience of adolescence as 'that intense, suspended moment between yesterday and tomorrow, between childhood and adulthood, between being nobody and a somebody, when everything is in question, and anything is possible' (2011: 112).

As the coming-of-age films are not bound by characters' ages, target audiences, or stylistic conventions, we thus find it useful to follow a discursive approach to study these films as a sub-category of youth films. The term's connotation of transitioning, specifically from childhood to adulthood, allows us to discuss local and global examples – including *Mustang* – within this category, which centralise thematic concerns such as the joys and pains of growing up, generational conflicts, and rites of passage that vary in terms of culture, age, class, race, and gender. In this book, we pay particular attention to female coming-of-age as *Mustang* sits well with its sister films from Turkey and other national contexts of youth film. Although 'girl' and 'girlhood' are seemingly useful terms and have vast importance in their suggestive distinctions – which are also apparent in the growing literature on girl/girlhood studies – we often refrain from using them because of their different meanings in the Turkish context. In Turkish language, the use of 'girl' is loaded with sexist and moralist connotations as it traditionally refers to a single woman, and since a single woman is 'assumed' to be a virgin, it also refers to virginity. Therefore, different from English language wherein 'girl' refers to 'not adult', it refers to a girlhood without sexual experience in a Turkish traditional cultural context (Turner 2006).[4] Even though this heavy connotation is tending to fade out in certain segments of society, it is still prevalent and binding for the rest. As such, the then Prime Minister Erdoğan (now President) used it as an implied insult against a protester in Hopa in 2011, saying 'I do not know if it was a girl or a woman but she had climbed over a panzer' ('Turkey's President …' 2017), redundantly referring to her non-virginity. As is clearly seen from this example, the use of 'girl' or 'woman' is also closely related to gender politics in the Turkish context. In fact, purposive uses of 'woman' – regardless of its traditional meaning – in daily and public speeches have long been a significant act of feminist struggle in Turkey. Therefore, being mindful of this context, even when 'girl' and 'girlhood' are occasionally used throughout the book, it is crucial to note here that they do not invariably refer to the recognised thematic and conceptual connotations of girlhood studies.

Categorical Distinctions and Authorship

The question of categorising *Mustang* is both a subject matter and a methodological tool in this book. We attend to the ways in which its local and global reception locate the film within art-house world cinema, as well as problematise how it fits into and/or challenges the categorical notions of diasporic, migrant, and transnational filmmaking. Such an approach necessitates an analysis of how the filmic text engages with the socio-political context in Turkey, how it offers diverse positions from which to read it, and how local and global reception conceal this diversity by the restrictive codes of gender and nationality that the critics adopt in their reviews. We thus situate *Mustang* within discussions of transnational film as an anomalous example that calls for a reconsideration of essentialism in such categories.

Mustang was made by a filmmaker born in Turkey and based in France, within the context of a co-production among France, Turkey, and Germany; it was shown in several established festivals, and received awards by critics from reputable organisations. In this respect, the film is transnational in its creative and financial production, distribution, and reception, which allows it to be readily classified under 'world cinema', 'European cinema', or 'transnational cinema', apparent in festival selections and critical reviews. Even though academic writing on *Mustang* is limited, there is a similar tendency to situate it within discussions of its (trans)nationality (Cerrahoğlu 2019; Handyside 2019) and relate this to issues and complexities in representation. These widely used categorical terms to identify the film, along with 'art-house cinema' that the film is interpellated with, remain broad and ineffective in reading *Mustang*. Moreover, their routine use prompts us to review and clarify the definitions of how we use these terms here in order to reduce or eliminate ambiguities, and underline how we problematise them to a certain degree.

Naficy (2001) delineates his concept of accented cinema around the works of filmmakers that he groups as exilic, diasporic, and postcolonial ethnic filmmakers. Born in Ankara to Turkish parents, educated in Paris and Johannesburg, and settled in France, Ergüven is a migrant by choice, but her migrant identity is not a major criterion that shapes the narratives in her filmmaking practice. She spent the first few years of her life in Ankara. Her family moved to France due to her father's position as a diplomat when she was four years old. She was raised and educated mainly in France, while travelling back and forth to Turkey and willingly decided to stay in Paris with her sister before she graduated from a high school in France even though her parents had left. She got a master's degree in African history in Johannesburg before deciding to make a career in filmmaking and entered La Fémis. There she made two shorts *A Drop of Water* (2006) and *Mon trajet préféré* (2006), followed by her post-graduation feature debut *Mustang*. She is neither exiled nor belongs to the Turkish diaspora in France. Her ties with both countries are not strict or inflexible: as evident in her interviews, ethnicity and nationality are not discourses with which she defines her identity. Her story as a privileged migrant is singular and personal, rather than a consequence of a collective occurrence; and it is marked mainly by socioeconomic factors. Nonetheless, *Mustang* is a film about growing up as a young woman in Turkey, the country in which Ergüven was born, and it comprises some of the recurring themes Naficy identifies when defining 'accented cinema', such as home/homeland, familial attachments, and crises of belonging. Co-produced and co-written with an international group of filmmakers, the film's style resonates with examples of global art-house films, and interstitiality is something that governs its form and content. Ergüven reveals that the story is partly autobiographical, and it does pose questions relevant to belonging to a place. However, *Mustang*'s narrative and narration direct us to assess these questions within the national context rather than consider them within the tropes of accented and migrant filmmaking. The film also allows us to rethink these existing categories and evaluate whether they are potentially useful when analysing *Mustang*.

Mustang's hybridity is intricately attached to Deniz Gamze Ergüven's identity as a non-Western migrant woman filmmaker with multiple nationalities. The film, its production and funding processes, and its festival line-up decisions and critical reception are entangled phenomena that are mutually informed by one another and bound by Ergüven's 'palatably foreign' (Marciniak 2007) authorship.[5] Her transnational identity, as well as the narrative and stylistic devices she uses, as mentioned above, are incompatible with the essentialist categorisations of migrant and diasporic cinema. However, as an up-and-coming 'Turkish-French' female auteur from Europe, her work can be located within a transnational body of filmmaking by women with similar stories of mobility. In her work on *Women's Cinema, World Cinema* (2015), Patricia White writes about diverse films from different countries of origin, made by women filmmakers whom she links under the umbrella of global festival circulation, and art-house distribution and funding networks. The films she attends to reside in the categories of world cinema and transnational cinema, and they are inspired by and studied within a range of different feminisms. She writes:

> I contextualise the concept of women's cinema historically as both an explicitly feminist counter-cinema by and for women and as a critical discourse in academia. Feminist media culture has always been multi-sited, and its joint focus on production and critique means that the histories of women's filmmaking and of feminist politics and scholarship are intertwined. However, as a transnational formation, contemporary women's cinema draws on many

other histories – those of art cinema; national media industries; and a range of aesthetics, intellectual, and political movements, including feminisms, outside the Anglo-American context in which feminist film studies arose. Thus, I turn next to the burgeoning field of world and transnational cinema studies to evaluate how the axes of gender and sexuality can remap its concerns.

(2015: 8)

White's methodological approach to such films is instructive for our study of *Mustang*. Through discussions of works by Lucrecia Martel, Samira Makhmalbaf, and Deepa Mehta among others, she examines authorship within the politics and economics of critical reception as much as art-house funding and distribution, which determine a film's festival destinations, screenings, and value. White argues that 'a feminist orientation positions women's films in relation to discourses of agency (authorship) as well as aesthetics (representations), in terms of the politics of location as well as place of origin' (15), and that '"Woman" is as frequently associated with national ideologies in film as in other forms of politics, and feminist approaches must tease apart competing representations and self-representations' (16). In this respect, reading criticism on *Mustang* and Ergüven's interviews about the film and her filmmaking has a formative function to understand the gendered construction of her (trans)national identity evident in the language used and symptomatic of a common attitude towards art-house women filmmakers whose films circulate globally. Writing about the Iranian Farabi Cinema Foundation's objection against the film *Persepolis* (Satrapi 2007) and its participation in Cannes, White notes how 'Satrapi's attempt to negotiate questions of national identity and self-representation in *Persepolis* was [...] appropriated as a statement of the progressiveness of French culture' (16). The reception of Deepa Mehta's *Fire* (1996) was shaped by nationalism as there were 'claims that lesbianism was not Indian and [Mehta was] an inauthentic Indian filmmaker' (84) because she resided in Canada (see also Gopinath 2005: 131–60). The success of *Caramel* (Labaki 2007), on the other hand, 'was appropriated to discourses of the nation, softening Lebanon's image through the female director's humanizing perspective' (White 2015: 121). These examples speak to one another as they illuminate how migrant/diasporic women's cinema is perceived within the frames of foreignness and femininity, and how it is instrumentalised in art-house marketing and promotion rhetoric. *Mustang*'s transnational production, global circulation, style, and subject matter, along with its director's interstitial identity, renders it a similar case. Scrutinising the figure of the woman director allows us to ask questions pertinent to nationalism, gender politics, and the criticism of *Mustang*'s aesthetics. It also releases the potential complexities that the filmic text offers from what it has been categorically reduced to.

Mustang is a transnational production that centralises on a story taking place in Turkey with specific references to the Turkish political and social context. Yet, the film's formal strategies make it comparable to contemporary examples of European art-house cinema. Ergüven benefits from the nuances of global youth film aesthetics rather than investing in the realism-informed stylistic trends that dominate the cinema of Turkey (especially its rural *taşra*-themed films). *Mustang* should be approached primarily stripped of the rigid nationalities associated with the film and the filmmaker, which filter the film's potentialities. The film's subject and style prompt us to divide *Mustang*'s analysis into three chapters: the first one deals with contextualising the film in Turkey, the second one concentrates on its stylistic excess, and the third chapter engages with its local and global reception.

Outline

'A critical transnationalism', Higbee and Lim assert, 'must [...] be attendant to the dynamics of the specific historical, cultural and ideological contexts in the production and reception of each particular film' (2010: 12–13; see also Lim 2019). In line with this, we contend that the methodological tools in film studies should be revisited and diversified to produce nuanced accounts of transnationalism. Thus, a multi-scalar methodological framework that combines form/style, context, and critical reception is needed to understand *Mustang*'s complex affiliations with the national and the transnational. Triangulating three analytical modes, we propose a model that aims to match the mobility of migrant filmmaking practices with a migratory ethic of film criticism. Evading the dominant stylistic paradigms of Turkish cinema, and spectacularising willful femininity in response to the global revival of youth films, *Mustang* constitutes a powerful case study to examine new forms of migrant/interstitial filmmaking with revised methodological and conceptual tools. An effectively critical account of interstitial media practices and their semiotic dynamism requires a multi-scalar methodological framework that 'operates within and beyond a national referent', and 'constructs a reciprocal non-hierarchical relation between [...] local and global modes of intelligibility' (Çakırlar 2011: 361; 2013).

Our framework treats youth as a significant operational ground of affirmative ethics that moves the figures of world cinema from objects of victimhood to subjects of will. 'Affirmative ethics', Rosi Braidotti argues, 'locates the constitution of subjectivity in the interrelation to others, which is not only a form of exposure, availability and vulnerability, but also a mutually empowering relation' (2008: 7–8). Contesting the 'tendency of much contemporary ethical theory to focus primarily on melancholia, mourning and negativity', Braidotti's Spinozist account of joyful affirmation imagines a relational subject whose potentialities cannot be reduced to rigid identitarian regimes. 'Affirmative ethics', Braidotti asserts, 'assumes that humanity does not stem from freedom from the burden of negativity but rather that freedom is extracted out of the awareness of limitations' (35). Rather than assessing *Mustang* as a problem of identity, or as a cultural text impossible to translate, we propose an affirmative approach to the ways in which the film's engagement with youth mobilises, in celebrating or antagonising or even obscuring, different archives of will and willfulness in national, transnational, and diasporic/migrant cinemas. Choosing to locate the subject of coming-of-age, and the on-screen representations of her will, in the very centre of our work allows us to explore critically the possibilities and limitations of feminist affirmation in transnational frameworks of film aesthetics and criticism. *Mustang*'s affirmation of willful youth as a *dispositif* of transnationalism encourages us to revisit the familiar methodological tools of film studies to be able to engage, more expansively, with the film's cross-cultural mobility.

The three chapters of the book are organised according to the three modes of analysis we identified for our approach to the film. In the first chapter, titled 'Escaping New Turkey's "Wife Factory": Towards a Contextualisation of the Claim for Female Voice and Subjectivity', we discuss the film's engagement with gender politics in contemporary Turkey. In the last two decades, Turkey has been going through a massive change in line with the 'New Turkey' project of AKP, wherein the politics of gender and sexuality plays a central role. Especially since the 2011 elections, women's bodies and sexualities have been used as the main discursive ground to maintain and promote socio-cultural regulation. The increasing and strikingly overt tone of anti-feminism in the discourses and policies of the AKP government paved the way for the marginalisation of women's rights, promotion of familialism, and normalisation of gender-based violence. In this respect, some scholars even suggest that a new gender order, or a new mode of patriarchy, is at stake (Coşar and Yeğenoğlu 2011). Meanwhile, as opposed to the rising voice of this new order, which defines women's agency and values of femininity merely in the domain of the familial, new women's narratives that reclaim agency and subjectivity on the screen have shown a remarkable increase in contemporary Turkish cinema. In stark contrast to the

Introduction 19

distinctive characteristics of the previous two decades of male-centred narratives, which prioritise male agency and points of view at the cost of silencing or casting out their female characters, these emergent narratives bring forward female agency and visual and narrative authority, as well as new ways of storytelling. Following up these two trajectories, this chapter aims to put forth a reflection on the contextual associations of *Mustang*'s cinematic imagination of youth, gender, and sexuality. The film's narrative revolves around familial and societal gender-based violence, oppression, and abuse: it uses cinematic devices to claim female voice and narrative authority, and has direct and allegorical references to the changing socio-political context in Turkey. Therefore, *Mustang* stands at a suggestive ground that reveals and enables us to reflect on the close link between the recent cinematic trends in contemporary Turkish cinema and the changing socio-political climate in a country that makes itself mostly apparent in authoritarian, anti-feminist, and conservative discourses.

The second chapter, titled 'Framing the Willful Subject of Coming-of-Age: Cinematography and Stylistic Excess', focuses on the ways in which style and textuality operate in the film's representation of gender, dissent, and coming-of-age. Through its expressive use of *mise-en-scène* and cinematography, *Mustang* constructs a globally intelligible space to depict gender-based violence and resistance, where the national reference and its local political intricacies are located in details such as the mediated noises preaching moral values on TV (with references to news and soap operas) and the #DirenGezi (famous slogan of Gezi Park protests, meaning 'ResistGezi') print on a t-shirt briefly shown on screen. In the film's presentation of the domestic space and the five protagonists' alignments with it, the melodramatic tropes are dramatically at play: the film registers the immobility-flight, inside-outside, private-public, and rural-urban binaries to highlight the hegemonic relations within the gendered and segregated operations of space. Throughout the film, windows, doors, and fences are where the boundaries of this gendered spatiality dissolve and the possibility of resistance appears. This chapter argues that *Mustang*'s stylistic register – which seems to privilege the musculature/rhythm of the moving image, a mid-brow art-house 'look' through its cinematography, and especially the *mise-en-scène*, including the expressive uses of colour, costumes, and landscape/settings – works to construct a transnational feminist optic. This feminist optic makes the dissident girlhood on screen palatable to international audiences. This chapter also questions the ways in which this transnational film aesthetic allows diverse interpretations both in local and global political contexts. The excess in the film's expressive style, we argue, informs significantly the discursive divisions in its critical reception.

Mustang's reception is seemingly shaped by the reviewers' understanding of national identity, gender, and sexuality in Turkey. While its global reception revolves around the idea that this is a well-written, well-directed and highly stylised film that exposes the repression of women in general through a simple story taking place in a remote village in Turkey, local critics rate the film as average and are focused mainly on the issues surrounding the representation of reality. Rather than paying attention to the details of the fictional world and its coherence, local critics generally evaluate the film through its references to real-life occurrences and experiences, and through its loyalty to locations and characters as known in reality. *Mustang*'s global reception, on the other hand, is built on criticism that attends to the ability of Ergüven's handling of the film's subject matter, the appeal of which lies in its familiar feminist tones coming from characters from a remote setting. Through an analysis of Turkish, Anglophone, and Francophone reviews and criticism, the third chapter, titled 'Critical Reception: Paradoxes of National Belonging and Geopolitics of Film Criticism', looks at themes stemming from the differences between the film's reception in Turkey and abroad. Moreover, this chapter provides a discussion of the film's narrative elements such as setting, time, characters, and dialogue as well as its stylistic choices including editing, sound, and camerawork, and explores the different viewpoints about youth, feminism, and nationalism evident in the film's reception.

Notes

1 Regarding the representation of traumatic past through the uses of child figure in the post-millenial cinema of Turkey, see also Atakav (2014).
2 For a close reading of *Hayat Var* in relation to coming-of-age narratives in Turkish cinema, see also Düzcan (2017)
3 The significant use of *arabesk* music in the film points at a stylistic expression of Hayat's willfull presence. *Arabesk* music is a popular genre that reflects migrant subculture in modern urban life. The association of this genre, which is loaded with highly masochistic and macho sensibility, with a young female teeneger's wanderings alone in the city subverts the gendered codes of the *arabesk* culture (Güçlü 2011).
4 As opposed to 'girl', 'boy' is rarely used for referring to 'not adult' and does not ascribe the feature of male virginity in the Turkish context (see also Turner 2006; Bozkurt 2014).

5 Ergüven's 'palatable foreignness' moves to a different direction with the production and reception of her second feature *Kings* (2017). She spent a couple of years in Los Angeles writing the script of *Kings* before she started working on *Mustang*. It was Alice Winocour, her co-writer for *Mustang*, who advised her to start with another film to be able to fund the *Kings* project. *Mustang* was both a success at the box office and international festivals and competitions, including an award at Cannes and an Oscar nomination by France for the Best Foreign Language Film. Filmed in the US and starring Halle Berry and Daniel Craig, *Kings* was quite divergent from *Mustang*'s art-house production. The film is about the 1992 Los Angeles riots, which seemingly 'baffled investors, who couldn't understand why a French-Turkish helmer might be pitching such a story' (Debruge 2015). It is evident from her interviews that funding is more easily available to stories pertinent to a first-time filmmaker's identity. *Kings* was not rated highly amongst critics and viewers, and was criticised as unfocused and unguided in terms of story structure and real-life references (IMDb user reviews, Bradshaw 2017; Henderson 2018). Since then, Ergüven has moved onto directing television series, including two episodes of the much-debated show *The Handmaid's Tale* in 2019.

1 Escaping New Turkey's 'Wife Factory'

Towards a Contextualisation of the Claim for Female Voice and Subjectivity

With its narrative revolving around familial and societal gender-based violence, abuse, and patriarchal oppression of the young, *Mustang* is a film about growing up as a woman in Turkey. 'No matter how you look at it', the director Deniz Gamze Ergüven states, 'the film reveals certain realities of Turkey' (Gürcü 2015a).[1] In almost every interview, while discussing the storyline or characters, and explaining the motivations behind her filmmaking practice, Ergüven makes various references to contemporary Turkish socio-political context, and its gender politics in particular. This engagement also becomes uniquely apparent in the diegetic world with direct references, most striking of which are the televised voice-offs of Turkey's former Prime Minister (now President) Recep Tayyip Erdoğan and of former Deputy Prime Minister Bülent Arınç delivering speeches on sacred motherhood, 'ill-mannered' feminists, and female chastity. Accordingly, it is not the omnitemporal 'realities of Turkey', but the ones that epitomise Erdoğan's increasingly anti-feminist, authoritarian, and conservatist project of 'New Turkey' that are of concern. Moreover, the director also states that 'it's a film that treats a gloomy reality, but with hope and strength' and adds: 'there's something about the resilience of these girls' (quoted in Kilkenny 2017). Throughout the film, *Mustang*'s young sisters stand up, as willful subjects, against all the calls of this project of 'New Turkey' in their own distinctive ways at all costs, and mostly with joy, laughter, and self-determination. That is supported by a style that spectacularises willfulness and prioritises the youngest sister Lale's visual and narrative authority. Female youth pervades the screen by all means, which operates in stark contrast to the codes and conventions of the previous two decades of male-centred narratives in Turkish cinema, which tended to prioritise male points of view along with masochistic subtexts (Arslan 2009) characterised by a highly melancholic tone (Akbal Süalp 2009).

DOI: 10.4324/9781003089056-2

Furthermore, *Mustang* also remains, to some extent, at odds with the newly emergent women-centred narratives in the contemporary Turkish cinema. It is in line with them in terms of reclaiming female voice, agency, and subjectivity on the contemporary Turkish cinema screen, but still diverges from them with its style and direct references to the political context. In this regard, *Mustang*'s affiliation with contemporary cinema of Turkey is controversial. Its affirmative claim for willful youth does not sit in complete harmony with the dominant narrative and stylistic patterns of gender representation in the cinema of Turkey. Its cinematic expression of and claim for young female subjectivity, voice, and agency strongly resonates with the context of 'New Turkey', while the film attempts to go beyond the national cinema's predictable scripts of gender-based violence that primarily invest in various registers of realism. This diversion not only explains the film's polarised critical reception but also mobilises a new grammar of understanding dissent in Turkey. Hence, *Mustang* can be considered as a timely and willful cinematic response to growing up as a woman in 'New Turkey', which plots an escape from 'New Turkey's "wife factory"'.

However, we argue that this strong contextual affiliation is frequently mentioned but loosely discussed, or not elaborated adequately. Instead, both *Mustang*'s and the director Ergüven's national identity and belonging come to the fore and are thoroughly disputed as significant issues defining the critical reception of the film. The film's stylistic features converge on global coming-of-age narratives (rather than on Turkish youth films) and its Oscar nomination for France's entry for Best Foreign Language Film, along with its critical acclaim in the international festival circles, might have facilitated this odd identity quest, which results in often conflicting evaluations of the film. For instance, the film was labelled 'disturbingly orientalist' (Ercivan 2015) and 'an exemplary of objectifying male gaze' (Özakın 2015) but also a 'portrayal of Turkish women's reality' (Beardmore 2016) and 'a feminist statement' (Clarke 2016). While we further explore the film's reception later in the book, this chapter aims to put forth the film's close engagement with contemporary political and cinematic contexts in Turkey, paying particular attention to gender politics. To interpret and go beyond existing binary oppositions revolving around *Mustang* and its critical reception (East/West, Muslim/secular, traditional/modern, rural/urban, liberation/oppression, authentic/orientalist, etc.), we deem it crucial to place it in dialogue with the Turkish context. In doing so, this chapter will unpack the possibilities of multi-layered, more nuanced, diverse, and even contradicting positions and readings that the film calls forth regarding the representation of female youth and subjectivity.

Changes in the Blink of an Eye: 'New Turkey' and Its 'Wife-Factory'

Mustang begins with a voice-over of the youngest sister Lale, also narrator of the film, saying: 'It's like everything changed in the blink of an eye. One moment we were fine, then everything turned to shit!' This is followed by the first scene, in which Lale is seen on the last day of school before summer vacation, giving a farewell hug to her beloved teacher who is leaving for Istanbul. On their walk home, the five sisters decide to go to the beach with male school friends, and they have a vibrant, youthful afternoon under the shining sun. Running on the beach, giggling, and splashing each other, and playing games in the water on their friends' shoulders, they greet the summer holidays with joy (see Figure 1.1). Then comes the incident causing the aforesaid sudden and irreversible transition in their lives.

When they go back home, they get punished for their supposedly obscene behaviour at the beach, 'rubbing up against boys' necks' in their grandmother's words. From this moment on, Lale's opening voice-over swiftly finds its meaning. They are beaten up, taken to hospital for virginity tests, and locked up. Anything that is likely to 'pervert' them – from mobile phones to make-up – is banned. The young sisters are stripped of any means of self-expression and communication with the outside world. Instead, the house becomes a 'wife-factory', as Lale describes it, to prepare them for becoming docile and diligent brides for their future husbands and families.

Affirming Lale's words literally, the narrative equilibrium is disrupted by this incident so rapidly and dramatically at the beginning of the film, causing a startling change in the sisters' lives. In

Figure 1.1 The sisters' play at the beach with their classmates in *Mustang*.

fact, some of the critics found such an abrupt change towards a 'wife factory' 'unconvincing' and even introduced that as a fallacy, a proof of the film's 'inauthenticity' or 'inappropriate' nonrealism (Aydemir 2015; Vardan 2015). However, this swift and profound transition is meaningful and very suggestive of the Turkish political context in the 2010s, particularly considering the rapid and dramatic change apparent in the governing party's policies and public discourses on gender and sexuality. After the third electoral victory with almost 50 percent of the vote in 2011, the AKP turned sharply away from its previous policy of democratisation and reformism in dialogue with women's rights organisations. The post-2011 period can be considered as a turning point in the AKP rule as the party started to set forth an overt authoritarianism, anti-feminism, and conservatism in the aftermath of its electoral hegemony. The new era, referred to by the AKP as 'New Turkey', was introduced to indicate that 'the social and political order under the party's rule is maintained by a new set of norms and values' (Korkut and Eslen-Ziya 2016: 13). This includes a new gender order, with 'a clear regression on gender equality and its role in the status of women' (Burul and Eslen-Ziya 2018: 180). In fact, the shift was so dramatic that some scholars even suggested that a new mode of patriarchy had been at stake (Coşar and Yeğenoğlu 2011). The party's new gender politics has mostly manifested itself as the marginalisation of women's rights, domination of familialism, and normalisation of gender-based violence (Acar and Altunok 2013; Öztan 2014; Kandiyoti 2016). Meanwhile, the post-2011 period in Turkey has witnessed former Prime Minister Erdoğan's call for 'at least three children' per family ('Turkish PM Erdoğan Reiterates ...' 2013), his declaration of not believing in gender equality as men and women are different 'in nature' (*fıtrat*) ('Turkish President Erdoğan Says Gender...' 2014), his advice to female students of not delaying marriage ('Evliliği geciktirmeyin ...' 2014), and his consideration of abortion as 'murder' ('Abortion is Murder ...' 2012). In this context, the government penned new legislations and regulations in favour of familialism, such as marriage allowances, marriage incentives for university students, pre-marriage counselling services, heterosexual-married-couple-only approach of assisted reproduction technologies and bans for third-party assisted reproduction. Along with these developments, the AKP 'defines the familial sphere as the natural locus of women' (Coşar and Özkan-Kerestecioğlu 2017: 162).

Moreover, in 2011, the Ministry of Women and Family Affairs was replaced with the Ministry of Family and Social Policies. With this significant change, it is registered that women, on the institutional level, are not recognised in society outside the familial domain. Yet, the familial domain is defined by an 'explicitly heteronormative-patriarchal family notion, biological determination and disciplining sexuality' (Öztan 2014: 182). Women who do not fit in or oppose this definition are often targeted and/or exposed to discrimination by government officials. For instance, women who refuse maternity are deemed 'deficient and incomplete' by Erdoğan ('Turkish President Says "Childless" ...' 2016). Divorced women, as 'family-breakers', do not receive any assistance from the government, while widowed women are financially supported (Öztan 2014: 181). Lesbian, bisexual, trans and queer women's existence is either denied ('Turkish President Erdoğan Says There is ...' 2021) or subjected to hate speech ('Efkan Ala da hedef gösterme ...' 2015; '"We do exist" ...' 2021) by the representatives of the government. While Former Minister of Women and Family Affairs Aliye Kavaf declared that 'homosexuality is a biological disorder, a disease' ('Homosexuality is ...' 2010), her successor, then Minister of Women and Family Affairs Fatma Şahin stated that it is her duty to take protective measures against 'family-breaker concepts', that is, LGBTQ+ people ('The AKP's LGBTI ...' 2015). In this regard, while 'family-breakers' of all sorts are marginalised, women are rendered to familial roles of being mothers and wives (Coşar and Yeğenoğlu 2011; Acar and Altunok 2013; Öztan 2014; Cindoglu and Unal 2016; Eslen-Ziya and Kazanoğlu 2022). Indeed, along with the 'New Turkey' project, the country under AKP rule – recalling Lale's words – has become a 'wife factory'.

While the 'wife factory' of Turkish political context designates home as the proper place for a 'proper woman', who is defined by being a housewife and serving the heterosexual family unit with unquestioned obedience (Atuk 2020: 290), it also incentivises marriage at an early age aiming to control female sexuality (Cindoglu and Unal 2016). Likewise, *Mustang*'s domestic confinement of the sisters in their 'wife factory' comes with routine daily tutorials of traditional housewife tasks taught by village 'aunties'. To be 'ideal' wives for their near future husbands, they have to learn housecleaning and sewing, and listen to the detailed instructions of making the best broth, stuffing *sarma* and rolling out dough for *mantı*. Besides this, outside the home, the 'wife factory' imposes a dress code upon the sisters. They are forced to wear long, shapeless, and in Lale's own words, 'shit-coloured' dresses instead of their colourful t-shirts, shorts, or jeans. This 'housewife home-schooling' (as the girls are removed from the school) is a preliminary step to quickly marry girls off one after another. Anything that could trigger youthful vibrant female sexual energy is to be covered with long, thick, brown fabrics, and with moral regulations of early marriage.

While 'policing gender norms and enforcing conservative family values constitute central nodes of AKP ideology' (Kandiyoti 2016: 105), women's bodies and sexualities are used in an unprecedented way as the main discursive tools of socio-cultural regulation (Acar and Altunok 2013; Cindoglu and Unal 2016; Korkman 2016). Turkey's ruling politicians, Erdoğan in the first place, made many scandalous public statements that define and promote a 'proper' womanhood conforming to the conservative, patriarchal, and neoliberal ethos of the 'wife factory' while casting out and/or stigmatising the ones who do not comply with it. For instance, echoing the reason behind the sisters' new dress code, a female TV presenter was sacked for wearing a low-cut top following the AKP's former spokesperson Hüseyin Çelik's remark that it was 'unacceptable' and 'extreme' ('Turkish TV Presenter ...' 2013). Another example that resonates with the ways in which *Mustang* addresses the oppressive forces of morality, chastity, and decency is Erdoğan stating that co-ed student housings were against conservative norms and the values of society ('Over Half of Turks ...' 2013) and that it was the duty of the state to intervene and protect the youth from 'all manners of dubious activities' ('Erdogan Wants ...' 2013). The former Minister of the Interior Muammer Güler took it a step further and argued that co-ed student housings were hubs of illegal activities such as prostitution ('Over Half of Turks ...' 2013). As seen in these examples, even though some critics of the film find the dramatic change in the sisters' lives unconvincing or unrealistic, the 'wife factory' that *Mustang*'s sisters live through seems to cohere with both the swiftness and the extent of the change in the status of women imposed by the 'New Turkey' project. It also aligns with the rising conservative, familialist, heteronormative, and anti-feminist discourses, morals, values, and policies that aim to regulate women's lives, bodies, and sexualities.

Catherine Driscoll suggests that the narrative of teen films centres on obstacles, which operate through the tension between coming-of-age and maturity: 'Maturity is a question and a problem within teen film rather than a certain set of values. [...] [T]een film is less about growing up than about the expectation, difficulty, and social organisation of growing up' (2011: 66). Within this context, *Mustang* may not easily pass as a teen film. However, it engages with the codes of the genre subversively through its displacement of pivotal motifs, such as young heterosexuality, virginity, intergenerational conflicts, and institutional management of youth by families (2). For instance, the prominent generic motif of 'summer holiday' as the transitional space, where changes start in most teen films or coming-of-age narratives (70), is used in *Mustang* not to invoke freedom from the social constraints of school, but rather to emphasise confinement, the swift transition of the sisters' lives in the 'wife factory'. Thus, living through the 'wife factory' is cast as the difficulty, that is, the main narrative obstacle itself. Yet, rather than merely complying with transnational generic features, these motifs are employed in *Mustang* to engage with the difficulty of growing up as a woman in New Turkey. This becomes even more explicit as *Mustang* also intentionally and directly ties itself with the discursive gender regime of New Turkey by inserting two well-known examples of the abovementioned public statements in its diegetic world.

'No' to 'Wife Factory'! 'No' to 'Proper' Womanhood!

In the scene where Ece is eating the 'arranged marriage' cookies almost mechanically on the kitchen counter, the televised male voice is heard saying:

> I used to kiss the soles of my mum's feet. She made a fuss about it. I said Mum, don't pull your feet away. That's the fragrance of paradise. Sometimes she cried. That's how mothers are. Some will understand, others won't. Feminists won't. They refuse motherhood.

The other televised statement in the film comes shortly after, in one of the key scenes where the whole family have their lunch around the dining table watching the news. A male televised voice is heard saying:

> Women must be chaste and pure, know their limits and mustn't laugh openly in public or be provocative with every move. Women must guard their chastity. Where are the girls who blush when you look at them?

Although these may sound fictional or unrealistic for an audience who is unfamiliar with the post-2011 Turkish political context, the former statement is actually an excerpt from Erdoğan's speech at the Women and Justice Summit in 2014, where he also declared that gender equality was against nature ('Turkish President Erdoğan Says Gender...' 2014). The latter is part of a speech in which former Deputy Prime Minister Bülent Arınç complains about women's 'moral decline' during a Ramadan Feast meeting in 2014 ('Women should not ...' 2014). The use of these off-screen voices not only sets the film's time-space in 2014, but also locates the house-as-'wife factory' within the 'wife factory' of 'New Turkey'. Almost as a vocal ghost haunting the diegetic world, the socio-political context does not find its direct image/body but leaks inside the house through these voice-offs, while setting forth the extent of sexist public statements of the AKP's prominent political figures that serve to promote a 'proper' womanhood. What is also striking is that *Mustang* associates these moralist and anti-feminist statements primarily with Ece, the only sister who cannot survive the 'wife-factory' as she commits suicide. Through this association, it points at the fatal and violent implications of the gender politics of 'New Turkey' for the ones who do not fit in.

In her article on femicides and the political rhetoric in Turkey, Sumru Atuk (2020) asserts that there is a close relationship between the sexist political statements and increased gender-based violence in the AKP's 'New Turkey'. She introduces the concept of the 'speaking state'. Accordingly, the ever-increasing sexist political statements contribute to a violent gender regime by proclaiming 'proper' gender-normative behaviours for women, therefore justifying violence towards noncomplying performances of femininity (Atuk 2020: 284). Referring to both Erdoğan's and Arınç's abovementioned speeches, Atuk argues that these statements promote modesty as the standard of women's propriety and target women who refuse to comply with gender norms, therefore explaining and justifying gender-based violence by moral decay (291–2). In the same vein, Deniz Kandiyoti (2016) also argues that the AKP's gender politics serve to normalise gender-based violence by constantly creating exclusionary boundaries between modest 'us' and immoral 'them'. Only 'proper women', '(our) deserving (sisters) are worthy of protection, the rest, and especially those with the audacity to break the norms of modesty and protest in public put themselves in jeopardy' (Kandiyoti 2016: 106).

At first glance, Ece's suicide may not directly be put into the category of femicide or gender-based violence; however, it is clear that she kills herself as she does not want to fit in, and collides with the category of 'proper' womanhood. Just before Ece's suicide, while Uncle Erol is watching, attentively and seriously, Arınç's speech on the news, Ece makes her sister laugh by her obscene gestures and disregard for Erol's warnings – 'shush!' After Erol bursts with anger and asks her to leave the table, Ece goes to the kitchen and kills herself with her uncle's gun. By setting the suicide scene against the voice of a leading political figure representing 'New Turkey' and calling on women for modesty and docility, *Mustang* not only proclaims the fatal role of the AKP's gender politics in women's life on the screen, but also asserts the suicide as a disobedient and willful response to that. Against the moralising voices of both the uncle and Arınç (representing the Uncle of the state) shushing women's laughter, Ece claims for her disobedient voice in her own way, yet at the cost of her total exclusion by death. Nevertheless, Ece's suicide still registers her presence, agency, and ultimate protest in the film: her unexpected and shocking action evades the moralising and silencing male voices and pervades the diegesis with the sound of her gunshot.

It is crucial to note here that *Mustang* does not victimise its young female characters though revealing all the violent and startling workings of the 'wife factory'. Throughout the narrative, the sisters struggle against it in their own way, and mostly in solidarity. Thus, if *Mustang* tells the difficulty of growing up as a woman in New Turkey, it also powerfully articulates and exposes the young sisters' rage against and defiance of its norms of 'proper' womanhood. Nur breaks the chairs in the garden and cries out to her grandmother after learning that Petek Hanım informs on them. Lale confronts Petek Hanım and yells at her: 'do your shit-coloured dresses make you everyone's moral judge?' Sonay 'improves', in her words, long, shapeless, shit-coloured dresses and rips her skirt. Lale spits on the coffees prepared for Ece's betrothed. When they are under house confinement, Sonay breaks the ban several times and escapes through her window to meet her boyfriend. The five sisters sneak out of the house to watch a football match in the city as Uncle Erol does not give them permission. At the risk of her life, echoing Ece's suicide, Selma says to the doctor that she slept with the entire world when she is taken for a virginity test on her wedding night. Moving beyond the dichotomies of oppression-victimisation/freedom-emancipation, *Mustang* renders them complicated, and features the sisters' voices and their reckless responses. Later in this chapter, and in the following one, we discuss this in more detail in relation to the film's political context and its cinematography and style, respectively. Yet, it is still important to briefly note here that these sisters' oppositional behaviours are not merely reactionary, they contest and collide with the patriarchal figures of the 'wife factory' and its gender norms. Thus, it is in fact the acts of these patriarchal figures that are reactionary: they respond, each time with increasing violence, to the sisters' noncomplying behaviours to assert their authority. This also evokes Kandiyoti's conceptualisation of 'masculinist restoration' (2016: 109) with regards to the emergent forms of gender-based violence and rising marginalisation of women's rights in the AKP's New Turkey. As Kandiyoti suggests, 'women's rising aspirations and determined male resistance create a perfect storm in gender order that manifests itself in both semi-official attempts to "tame" women and uphold men's privileges [...] and in the unofficial excesses of street-level male violence' (2016: 110). Accordingly, any severe and violent attempt to control the sisters' lives is in fact the consequence of the perfect storm that they cause in gender order, again and again, throughout the narrative.

Mustang's emphasis on women's rebellion and resistance also evokes the oppositional voices in the socio-political realm raised by feminists, LGBTQ+ activists, non-governmental organisations, public figures and through public protests. For instance, thousands of women marched against Erdoğan's anti-abortion bill in 2012; and mocked Arınç's abovementioned statement on women's laughter in 2014 through posting laughing selfies in social media. Feminists and LGBTQ+ activists have been protesting against the AKP's 'politics of intimate' (Acar and Altunok 2013). As Zeynep Korkman suggests,

> feminists and queer social movements have been the most vocal critics of neoconservative familialism [...] Feminist and queer activists objected to the promotion of heteronormative, marital, reproductive sexuality as a government endorsed norm, to the intensified demand placed upon women to marry and reproduce, [...] demonstrating that there are multiple desires for intimacy and domesticity that are not centred around a married heterosexual couple and their biological children.
>
> (2015: 352)

Besides this, women have been raising their voices for years through public protests and social media campaigns against dramatically increasing male violence, femicide and transfemicide cases in Turkey. These oppositional voices resisted the authoritarian voice of the 'speaking state' and challenged, in particular, the legitimacy of the AKP government and its gender politics (Kandiyoti 2016; Korkman 2016; Coşar and Özkan-Kerestecioğlu 2017). The 'untamed' sisters of *Mustang* resonate considerably with women's oppositional voices in the socio-political realm. Within this context, too, the use of Erdoğan's voice-off targeting feminists, and Ece's disobedient behaviours in return, are particularly meaningful.

In this regard, the t-shirt with #DirenGezi (#ResistGezi) print, locked in grandmother's wardrobe along with other items assumed to 'pervert' them, is noteworthy as another direct reference to the political context. #DirenGezi is one of the famous tags of anti-government Gezi Park protests in 2013, which united young people against the AKP's authoritarianism and patriarchal governance (Kandiyoti 2016; Çınar 2019). While 'exhibiting a worldview unimpressed with the dictums and slogans of political leaders striving to reshape the country and its youth', these protests 'marked the high point of a visibly defiant youth opposition to the AKP's power project' (Lüküslü 2016: 644). It is also striking that half of these people were young women (*Konda* 2014; Arat and Pamuk 2019). In many of her interviews, Ergüven also regards Gezi Park protests and women's resistance as inspiring. Ergüven's statements on the film's political references often invest in the rising political suppression in post-Gezi Turkey (Gürcü 2015b). In this respect, inserting such a pro-Gezi reference to its diegetic world, *Mustang* not only highlights the sisters' defiant opposition to the AKP's ideals of 'proper' youth, but also points to the post-Gezi climate of severe government repression, restriction, and censorship.

In this vein, *Mustang* responds to this repressive climate through the inclusion of these direct references. In addition, Ergüven reveals that the story has an autobiographical reference as the 'incident' that 'changed everything in the blink of an eye' in the narrative is something that she and her cousins once experienced when they were playing with their male friends (ibid.). Reflecting on her own experience in one of her interviews, she recalls her embarrassment and surrender to the blaming and lashing out that followed, while asserting the refusal of *Mustang*'s sisters to comply as heroic (ibid.). In this respect, *Mustang* also becomes Ergüven's belated response to the oppressive voices she once had to obey: a willful response, a 'No' to the 'wife factory'.

A Cinematic Response: Women's Rising Voices in Contemporary Cinema of Turkey

Especially through the significant uses of the abovementioned direct and indirect references, *Mustang* sets a unique example in its response to 'New Turkey'. The film is also meaningful and revealing within the context of new women's narratives that have emerged as a striking novelty in the cinema of Turkey. In the 2010s, films which were not necessarily directed by women but revolve around women protagonists, registering self-empowerment and self-realisation, showed a remarkable increase, and that stands in stark contrast to the distinctive characteristic of the previous two decades where male narratives come into prominence at the cost of silencing or scapegoating their female characters (Akbal Süalp and Şenova 2008; Akbal Süalp 2009; Suner 2010; Güçlü 2016). While Turkish cinema went through a striking change in the mid-1990s and a kind of rupture with the classical Turkish cinema's narrative patterns, style, and modes of filmmaking (canonised as 'New Cinema of Turkey'), one of the most notable aspects of this rupture is that this new wave of filmmaking was significantly shaped by male-centred narratives. Turkish cinema has always been a male-dominated arena in terms of narrative agency and point of view. However, beyond the divides of genre or authorship, 'the gender imbalance had never been so intense before in terms of representations and stories' (Güçlü 2016: 1). In fact, various film scholars describe the prominent examples of this new cinema as 'macho cinema' (Dönmez-Colin 2004: 64), or as 'male films' (Ulusay 2004: 144), or 'male weepy films' (Akbal Süalp 2009: 228). By placing male subjectivity at the centre of their narratives, these films, in various aspects, address masculinity more than ever before. Until the 2010s, through 'masochistic subtexts', they presented 'deviant' masculinities that defied male characters' authority and put classical masculinity in crisis (Arslan 2009: 259). Yet, these non-ideal representations of masculinities mostly presented self-pitying men whose victimhood needed redemption (Akbal Süalp 2009; Arslan 2009; Akbal Süalp 2014).

Female characters are subservient to these 'wounded' male characters and hold all the responsibility for their crises (Güçlü 2016). They 'become backdrops in most dramas [...] no meaningful dialogue [is] written for them' (Akbal Süalp and Şenova 2008: 92). If women are not completely silenced or excluded from the narrative, they are cast as 'morbid provocateurs and seducers who lead men to commit crimes, violence and irrational acts and who, of course, then become the victims of these brutalities' (ibid.). They are usually subjected to 'justified' graphic physical violence, abuse, and humiliation. As part of this masculinist picture, a distinct representational regime of gender difference emerged that framed women as silent, muted, and inaudible. From the mid-1990s till the 2010s, as a significant novelty, silent female characters were cast in several films, from box-office hits to art-house productions (e.g. *Eşkıya / The Bandit* [Turgul 1996], *Masumiyet / Innocence* [Demirkubuz 1997], *Gemide / On Board* [Akar 1998], *Uzak / Distant* [Ceylan 2002], *Asmalı Konak: Hayat / Ivy Mansion: Life* [Oğuz 2003] and *Romantik / Romantic* [Çetin 2007]). In these male-centred narratives, silent/silenced women function mainly as a tool through which male characters' points of view and experiences are revealed, and their discursive authorities are reassigned (Güçlü 2016). In most of these narratives, a gendered division of roles between the speaker (male) and the spoken-of (female) is created (ibid.) so that any potential cinematic appearance of women's narrative point of view, subjectivity, and agency is blocked.

Contrary to this cinematic picture, new women's narratives not only revolve around women protagonists with a strong emphasis on their agency, but also prioritise women characters' points of view and express their needs, desires, and anxieties. Moreover, most of these narratives, one way or another, engage with questions of women's empowerment, self-realisation, and subjectivity in Turkish society, in multiple trends and trajectories. *Mustang*, in terms of both time and content, and through distinctive formal choices, resonates with this cinematic context. A noteworthy trend appears in the increasing number of productions which revolve around complex women characters. A remarkable number of these examples foreground young women characters' resilience, self-realisation, or empowerment (e.g. *Mavi Dalga / The Blue Wave* [2013], *Kar / Snow* [2017]; *Tereddüt / Clair-Obscur* [2016], *Şimdiki Zaman / Present Tense* [2012], *Jîn* [Erdem 2013], *Sibel* [2018], *Nefesim Kesilene Kadar / Until I Lose My Breath* [2015]). As a counter-hegemonic response, these films constitute women's agency beyond the patriarchal boundaries of romance, marriage, and familialism, while also revealing the gender-based oppression and violence in these domains (e.g. *Şimdiki Zaman, Nar / Pomegranate* [Ünal 2011], *Kar, Zefir* [Baş 2010], *Jîn, Sibel, İşe Yarar Bir Şey / Something Useful* [Esmer 2017], and *Aşk, Büyü vs. / Love, Spell and All That* [Ünal 2019]). Echoing the sisters' willful 'no's to the oppressive rules and regulations of the 'wife factory' and their noncomplying representations in *Mustang*, a significant number of women characters in these narratives resist and respond to familial and gender-based violence, neglect, abuse, or oppression that they are subjected to (e.g. *Hayat Var, Kurtuluş: Son Durak / Last Stop: Kurtuluş* [Pirhasan 2012], *Sofra Sırları / Serial Cook* [Ünal 2017], *Tereddüt, Atlıkarınca / Merry-Go-Round* [Başarır 2010], *Nefesim Kesilene Kadar*, and *Ana Yurdu / Motherland* [Tüzen 2015]). As opposed to the male-centred narratives of the previous decade, women in these examples are not silenced, isolated, victimised, or scapegoated.[2]

Furthermore, contrary to the previous two decades' dominant representations of male bonding and/or hegemonic masculinity, these narratives inscribe women's deep and profound experiences of homosocial bonding as well as inter-generational conflicts and contradictions (e.g. *Kurtuluş Son Durak, Tereddüt, Ana Yurdu*, and *Köksüz / Nobody's Home* [Akçay 2013]). Among these examples, the rising voices of women directors, most of whom were making their first films, can be considered as another emergent trend. The practices of this new generation of women directors, we contend, reclaim female agency and subjectivity through their unconventional narratives (e.g. *Mavi Dalga, Ana Yurdu, Şimdiki Zaman, Köksüz, Zefir, Nefesim Kesilene Kadar, Toz Bezi / Dust Cloth* [Öztürk 2015], and *Hayaletler / Ghosts* [Okyay 2020]).

While *Mustang* differs from these examples in terms of both its distinctive non-realistic style (which we will discuss in more detail in the following chapter) and its direct references to Turkey's political context, it complies with these trends in terms of the abovementioned textual and authorial features. More importantly, it converges with their response to 'New Turkey's "wife factory"', to the AKP's familialist ideals of 'proper' womanhood. These films reinscribe 'improper' women's voices, desires, and agencies onto the Turkish cinema screen right at the time of the 'speaking state'. They can be considered as a timely cinematic response – very much resonating with women's protests and responses in the public domain – to the gender politics of 'New Turkey', with different cinematic ways of coping with it.

In this cinematic response, narrative focalisation is of crucial importance. As opposed to the previous decades of male-centred narratives, which literally silence their female characters, new women's narratives deliberately introduced and prioritised women's points of view through significant uses of voice and sound (e.g. *Hayat Var*, *Mavi Dalga*, *Şimdiki Zaman*, *İşe Yarar Bir Şey* and *Aşk, Büyü vs.*), through flashbacks (e.g. *Kurtuluş Son Durak*), through monologues (e.g. *Tereddüt, Atlıkarınca*), through visions, dreams, or imagination sequences (e.g. *Tereddüt, Sofra Sırları, Kar*), and through point of view shots (e.g. *Tereddüt, İşe Yarar Bir Şey* and *Nefesin Kesilene Kadar*). In this respect, *Mustang* stands out with its distinctive use of focalisation, most notably with its use of Lale's voice-over narration. In *The Acoustic Mirror*, Kaja Silverman asserts that '[the voice-over] inverts the usual sound/image hierarchy; it becomes a "voice on high", [...] a voice which speaks from a position of superior knowledge, and which superimposes itself "on top" of the diegesis' (1988: 48). In the same vein, Michel Chion argues in *The Voice in Cinema* that the acousmatic voice has complete power of seeing all and knowing all, it is omnipotent (1999). Accordingly, Lale's voice-over not only inscribes her point of view and subjectivity, but also presents her perspective as predominant. In other words, Lale's point of view is privileged in the story.[3]

Silverman argues that the voice-over's privilege loses its power and authority as it finds a localisation in the image, through embodiment (1988: 49). While the disembodied voice-over preserving its non-diegetic and non-corporeal character is exclusively male, female voice-over is exceptional, and eventually is anchored in the diegesis, and loses its power (48–9). At first glance, one may argue that Lale's voice-over is also situated in the diegesis and corporealised. However, as the voice-over narrates things that happened in the past (deliberately using past tense), her past image is anchored in the diegesis while her present image remains disembodied throughout the narrative. Here, Lale's voice-over sustains a temporal and spatial dislocation in the form of a temporal regression that positions the body of the voice as inaccessible since the real/present source of the voice is neither localised nor derived from a point within the diegesis. In fact, narrated from Lale's perspective, *Mustang* can be considered as an extended flashback of an escape from the 'wife factory' where the voice-over never finds its present source, and thus, exceptionally sustains its omnipresence. Mary Ann Doane suggests in 'The Voice in Cinema' that the voice-over during a flashback, 'very often simply initiates the story and is subsequently superseded by synchronous dialogue, allowing the diegesis to "speak for itself"' (1985: 168). However, as the whole film is constructed like a flashback, where the present source of the voice never converges with the image (therefore remaining inaccessible), Lale's voice-over in fact keeps hold of the narrative, rather than 'allowing the diegesis to speak for itself'. Against the distinctive use of the disembodied male voice-off of the 'speaking state' and its temporary authority on the diegesis, Lale's voice-over repeatedly and insistently cuts the story several times and inscribes her point of view, turning the narrative into a memory of her own, a story of her own.

This is also supported with the uses of other cinematic devices. Viewers not only hear but also see the whole story from Lale's perspective. Her visual point of view is prioritised through subjective shots. For instance, a distinctive use of point of view shots appears against the 'neighbour gaze', that is the controlling and intruding gazes on the sisters. In these moments, the image points to the controlling environment around the sisters, yet the visual authority is attributed to Lale as it is mostly seen from her point of view. In addition, the two embedded dream scenes, which provide the viewer with a glimpse of Lale's inner world, strengthen her narrative authority, establishing her subjectivity, desire, and agency further. These cinematic tools, once again, hold the narrative and make it a world of her own. With such distinctive formal choices in favour of its young female character's emotional interiority, voice and perspective, *Mustang* can be considered as a timely cinematic response to the male voices of Turkey's 'speaking state' that render women's lives and worlds merely objects of their pervasively sexist discourses and gender politics.

Escape Tools, Sewing a Life of Her Own: Claiming Joy and Hope

Within its subtle yet playful engagement with the national context, and its distinct cinematic response to gender-based violence, *Mustang* also insists on its affective mode, which differs from the majority of youth films in post-millennial Turkish cinema: making the narrative a world of Lale's own, the film asserts not only rage but also joy. Until Ece's suicide, nothing disrupts the sisters' joyful presence on screen. Despite confinement, violation, strict rules and regulations, they persistently create their own world with joy: they mock their 'shit-coloured dresses', swim on bedclothes, make catwalk shows, sunbathe in swimsuits, cheer and dance in a football match. Even after Ece's death, through Lale's dream scenes, the affect of joyful sisterhood manifests on screen. As opposed to the melancholic male characters of the new cinema of Turkey, *Mustang* projects the promise of the sisters' joy, giggles, and laughter onto the screen. The film performs affirmative politics by allowing the sisters to create a story, a world, a narrative of their own – rather than producing objects of victimhood.

Sara Ahmed begins her book *Willful Subjects* (2014) with the tale of the willful child by the Grimm Brothers. This is the story of a young girl's persistent disobedience and its violent costs:

> The willful child: she has a story to tell. In this Grimm story, which is certainly a grim story, the willful child is the one who is disobedient, who will not do as her mother wishes. If authority assumes the right to turn a wish into a command, then willfulness is a diagnosis of the failure to comply with those whose authority is given. The costs of such a diagnosis are high: through a chain of command (the mother, God, the doctors) the child's fate is sealed. It is ill will that responds to willfulness; the child is allowed to become ill in such a way that no one can 'do her any good'. Willfulness is thus compromising; it compromises the capacity of a subject to survive, let alone flourish.
>
> (Ahmed 2014: 1)

While Ahmed admits the power of the rod that 'straightens out' the child's arm in the story, an alternative account of subjectivity that takes more notice of the resistance of the willful arm is introduced. In this regard, Ahmed notes that willfulness is,

> A way of creating a space of one's own, of coming apart, or becoming apart from a structured and oppressive environment. Here 'ownness' is what allows a survival of 'belowness'. Willfulness or eigensinnig can be a way of withdrawing from the pressures of an oppressive world and can even become part of a world-making project. Willfulness as a diagnosis can thus be willingly inhabited, as a way of creating a room of one's own.
>
> (2014: 157)

Therefore, *Mustang*'s deliberate choice of taking a stand on the sisters' joy can be considered willing and willful in itself, that is, a way of carving out a space for themselves against oppressive forces. It is the expression of persistence on women's 'ownness', on creating a story/world/life/room of her own. That is why it is a film about a plan for escape from that oppression.[4]

It is about an insistence on creating a world of her own against the family, against the 'wife factory', against what is designated for her. That is registered not only by Lale's deliberate escape plan, but also by the sisters' willful persistence in creating their 'ownness' by 'stray[ing] from the official paths' of 'proper' womanhood in their 'own' way. Yet, with the successful escape of the youngest sisters, *Mustang* registers that it is 'premised on hope: the hope that those who wander away from the paths they are supposed to follow leave their footprints behind' (Ahmed 2014: 21). Like many of its sister women's narratives (e.g. *Tereddüt, Jîn, Kurtuluş Son Durak, Atlıkarınca, Ana Yurdu, Hayat Var, Sofra Sırları,* and *Sibel*), *Mustang* proposes a different intervention into the stories of oppression in Turkey. In an interview, the director Ergüven notes:

> What these girls do is what I dreamt I would have [done]. The choice conflates courage and hope – it's a film that treats a gloomy reality, but with hope and strength. There's something about the resilience of these girls. Even if I feel like I would not have had their strength in the same circumstances, it's a power that I recognise among us. It gives a body to the inner strength we have.
>
> (quoted in Kilkenny 2017)

The sisters, one way or another, evoke the possibility of a different story, that there is a chance to break apart, find alternative paths, rewrite, or say 'no' to the gender order. Therefore, the film not only serves to create a critical space for female subjectivity, but also proposes courage and hope for new possibilities.

However, the ending of *Mustang* also seems problematic in this respect as it obstructs more radical possibilities through the sheltering, or rescuing, closure that the teacher's embrace implies. The youngest sisters' escape to Istanbul ends up in the embrace of Lale's teacher (see Figure 1.2). This ending becomes particularly striking as the 'New Turkey' project is set against the Kemalist norms and values of the so-called 'Old Turkey' where the figure of the female teacher is one of the ideologically dense embodiments of 'Old Turkey's legacy of secular republicanism. While the modern and enlightened female teacher is attributed with the role of spreading the Republic's ideals of modern

Escaping New Turkey's 'Wife Factory' 39

Figure 1.2 Teacher's embrace at the final scene in *Mustang*.

secular state (especially to the 'uneducated' rural Anatolia), the girls' education and enlightenment are set as the key elements for the realisation of those ideals (Durakbaşa and Karapehlivan 2018). Therefore, the figure of the female teacher is very much associated with women's emancipation in Turkey's cultural history. Furthermore, the goal of 'New Turkey' in raising a 'pious generation' is aimed at undermining the Kemalist ideals of secularism, enlightenment, and modernisation that the female teacher figure embodies. This 'new myth of youth' is realised mainly through the Islamisation of national education (Lüküslü 2016) while renouncing gender equality (Durakbaşa and Karapehlivan 2018). Therefore, even though it is possible to argue that *Mustang* relies on women's solidarity and sisterhood in the end while being a party to women's emancipation, it fails, to a considerable extent, to escape reproducing the most hegemonic thus constitutive binary oppositions of Turkish politics that also shape the crises in Turkishness as national identity: secular vs. religious, modern vs. traditional; urban vs. rural.

Yet, despite these problematic connotations, unlike the female teacher – as the renowned embodiment of secular modernism – saving and liberating the youth from the rural 'backwardness', *Mustang*'s youngest sisters survive on their own, thanks to Lale's escape plan. Lale – not by coincidence, not by chance, not by accident, not by a momentary decision – delicately and willfully sews her escape plan and collects her escape tools throughout the narrative: she inspects possible exits from the house, finds the grandmother's money box, learns how to drive, and learns sewing for sleeping dummies. Her plan works, they run away from the shit-coloured clothes, from the 'wife-factory', from the destiny of marriage and obeying the state's familialist ethos of having 'at least three children'. They succeed and make it to Istanbul. With such a deliberately sewn plan, Lale claims the roads, the city, a life of her own. Yet again, 'ownness' becomes a part of world-making project in *Mustang*, to use Ahmed's terms.

Following Gilles Deleuze's thoughts on film 'as a consciousness of the world [provoking] a creative thinking *towards the world*, the unthought, the unseen' (quoted in Ceuterick 2020: 11), Maud Ceuterick suggests that 'filmic representation may present both a version of reality that seems fixed and immutable and the virtualities of the same reality' (11–12). In a similar vein, Jacques Rancière argues in 'The Paradoxes of Political Art' that artistic fictions have a huge potential in changing not only the consensual image of the world, but also our consensual way of relating to them:

> 'Fiction', as re-framed by the aesthetic regime of art, means far more than the constructing of an imaginary world [...] It is not a term that designates the imaginary as opposed to the real; it involves the re-framing of the 'real', or the framing of a dissensus. Fiction is a way of changing existing modes of sensory presentations and forms of enunciation; of varying frames, scales and rhythms; and of building new relationships between reality and appearance, the individual and collective.
>
> (2010: 141)

In this respect, *Mustang*'s persistence on joy and its hopeful claim for women's 'ownness', both through its narrative and formal choices, can be considered as an escape tool in itself. It brings out new possibilities and new paths to sight on screen, builds up new encounters, new ways of connecting to the world, new relationships between the gendered reality and its appearances. Echoing Ahmed's 'willful arm', it is like a cinematic disobedient 'arm' to New Turkey's 'rod', commanding women to 'know their place'. It willfully aims to alter the gendered realm of the possible.

Notes

1 All Turkish and French quotations and film titles were translated into English by the authors unless otherwise stated.
2 Some of these examples, including *Mustang*, are considered as embodying what Julia Kristeva conceptualised as 'intimate revolt' (Kristeva [1997] 2002; Çiçekoğlu 2019). Through this concept, Kristeva calls for a nonviolent culture of revolt taking place on the personal domain against social crises (precarity, racism, etc.) and personal crises (trauma, loss, apathy, etc.). Drawing upon

Kristeva's conceptualisation, Feride Çiçekoğlu suggests that such an intimate revolt of 'a new type of angry person' who wants the 'impossible' (Kristeva 2014: 1) can be traced in women characters of certain films made after the Gezi Protests in the contemporary cinema of Turkey (Çiçekoğlu 2019: 24). Accordingly, these films manifest a new type of beginnings through intimate revolts (ibid.).

3 This also contrasts with the male voice-over telling the story of Lisbon sisters in Sofia Coppola's *The Virgin Suicides* (1999). Even though the film's name was mentioned many times in comparison to *Mustang*, young female voice-over telling her own story stands as one of the crucial differences.

4 Regarding *Mustang* and *Sibel*, Delal Yatçi (2022) argues that willfulness becomes an escape door from these prison-like houses, and works like the female characters' power of flight. According to Yatçi, women directors in the contemporary cinema of Turkey depict home as a hell on earth, but nevertheless also pointedly imagine women's disobedience and solidarity that creates possibilities of escape from these houses.

2 Framing the Willful Subject of Coming-of-Age
Cinematography and Stylistic Excess

Focusing on an eclectic selection of films, including Alain Tanner's *Messidor* (1979), Claire Denis' *Vendredi Soir / Friday Night* (2002), Haifa al-Mansour's *Wadjda* (2012), and Fatih Akın's *Gegen die Wand / Head-On* (2004), Maud Ceuterick's study *Affirmative Aesthetics and Willful Women: Gender, Space and Mobility in Contemporary Cinema* calls for an alternative analytical framework in feminist film studies, one that addresses 'women's willful habitation of space along with a new vocabulary through which to theorise gender and space in film affectively' (2020: 1). 'What we need to examine', Ceuterick asserts, 'is not the "mobility" of these women but their bodily habitation of their spatial environments' (ibid). Shaped by Rosi Braidotti's 'ethics of affirmation' (2006; 2008) and Sara Ahmed's conceptualisation of 'willful subjects' (2014), the selection of films in this study represents 'women's spatial habitation' through an 'affirmative aesthetics', that is 'a cinematic way out of the restrictive dualistic oppositions that *freeze the present* into negative politics' (Ceuterick 2020: 5). Prioritising aesthetics and form rather than representation and narrative in film criticism, this framework bears the potential to 'enable the study of women's *micro-relations* to space through an 'affirmative' lens, examining their bodily and affective spatial relations rather than focusing upon the (lack of) "success" of their travel' (5). Interestingly, Ceuterick's case studies here do not address the intersections of gender and sexuality with age, although the 'willful' protagonists of *Messidor*, *Wadjda*, and *Head-On* are all young women whose (im)mobility shapes these films' aesthetic engagement with space and subjectivity. We thus argue that Ceuterick's intervention could operate as a powerful methodological tool to evaluate the 'willful mobility' of youth (or, of coming-of-age) in contemporary cinema.

As a transnational film and European co-production with multiple national affiliations, *Mustang* can be discussed in parallel to many

DOI: 10.4324/9781003089056-3

contemporary youth films, ranging from the globally acclaimed films such as Sofia Coppola's *The Virgin Suicides* (1999), Céline Sciamma's *Girlhood* (2014), and Sarah Gavron's *Rocks* (2019) to more 'local' examples of Turkish cinema such as Kutluğ Ataman's *2 Genç Kız / 2 Girls* (2005), Emine Emel Balcı's *Nefesim Kesilene Kadar / Until I Lose My Breath* (2015), Belmin Söylemez's *Şimdiki Zaman / Present Tense* (2012), Merve Kayan and Zeynep Dadak's *Mavi Dalga / The Blue Wave* (2013), Reha Erdem's *Hayat Var / My Only Sunshine* (2008), and Çağla Zencirci and Guillaume Giovanetti's *Sibel* (2018). These examples complicate the coming-of-age film as a distinct genre category as their engagements with style, genre, narrative, spectatorial address, and representational discourses of youth are diverse. The recent international revival of youth films in cinema and television also bears a similar heterogeneity, which complicates the treatment of coming-of-age as a genre. However, youth and coming-of-age, as themes, may operate as discursive tools to intervene into the ideological affiliations of style, genre, national cinema, and representation they operate in. Similarly, our analysis of *Mustang* treats the subject of coming-of-age as an ideologically complex thematic category that helps us locate its representations in aesthetic, political, and ethical terms.

Inspired by Ceuterick's affirmative approach to gender and space in film, we argue that coming-of-age films could be considered as what Sara Ahmed describes as a 'willfulness archive' (2014: 1). If 'willfulness', as Ahmed suggests, 'is a diagnosis of the failure to comply with those whose authority is given' (ibid.), then coming-of-age is bound to be a state of experiencing 'a relation between will and willfulness' that is characterised by the tension between the general will and the particular will (97). The condition of normative adulthood, according to Ahmed, is that 'the individual subject must learn to put aside his or her own particular or willful will and be willing to will the general will' (98). Hence, the subject of coming-of-age, who is always already a subject-in-process (e.g. the child and the adolescent), provides a fertile ground for a cinematic imaginary that engages with the drama of experiencing the gap between the general will and the particular will. In contradiction to a significant number of willful characters in Turkish coming-of-age films, *Mustang*'s style works to spectacularise willfulness in various forms, including those of disobedience, desire, escape, or passive volition. This stylistic excess, we contend, is one of *Mustang*'s core features, which leads to the film's polarised critical reception. As Chapter 3 will discuss in detail, most critics struggle with framing *Mustang*'s stylistic excess, which does not sit harmoniously with either the dominant trends of realism in contemporary Turkish cinema or the Eurocentric gaze that often objectifies the 'Third World' representations through the victim–survivor/oppression–emancipation dichotomies.

This chapter will provide an in-depth discussion of the role that *Mustang*'s style plays in registering the willful subject(s) of coming-of-age on screen. As the film's context of production, style, and representation troubles the established categories of 'national cinema', 'world cinema', 'European cinema', and 'transnational cinema', our analysis aims to match this paradox of national belonging by comparing *Mustang* with various coming-of-age films that play a significant role in setting the current trends of youth films in various contexts including contemporary Turkish cinema.

We will focus on the key formal components of the film, particularly characterisation, cinematography, narrative, and the *mise-en-scène*, including framing and the use of locations, settings, spatial tropes, and colour. Through a rigorous engagement with the film's aesthetic choices, this chapter will address the ways in which *Mustang* evades the ideological forces of national belonging in world cinema, and subverts its categorical default of realism in alternative/independent filmmaking. Implementing a comparative framework and positioning *Mustang* with the key national and international examples of the coming-of-age film, our analysis will demonstrate how the film's interstitial aesthetics, operating through Ergüven's binationality, substantially shapes the geopolitically marked differences in the film's critical reception.

Framing *Mustang*'s Five-Headed Creature

In the Q&A following the screening of *Mustang* at the French Institute Alliance Française (FIAF) in NYC, Deniz Gamze Ergüven notes that the five orphaned sisters of *Mustang* are 'one body with five heads, ten arms, ten legs', 'a monster femininity who loses one piece after another during the film, assesses wounds, re-composes, and strikes back' (FIAFNY 2016, see also Buder 2015). Here, Ergüven's account of the five sisters' on-screen presence assumes it as a spectacle of affirmative action and an embodiment of willful mobility. The director's approach to the body of femininity is a significant element of what we consider as *Mustang*'s stylistic excess. Rather than prioritising the emotional interiority and psychological depth of each sister, the film frames these five girls as a collective embodiment of willful mobility (see Figure 2.1). Resonating with Ceuterick's feminist framework, we argue that the subject of coming-of-age in *Mustang* '[produces] spaces and bodies that escape or suspend *fixed* ideas of gender and power-geometries' and 'bring[s] women's "mobility" under an "affirmative" light, by portraying

Framing the Willful Subject 45

Figure 2.1 *Mustang*'s five-headed 'Monster Femininity'.

their willful bodies' habitation of space-time in continual transformation' (2020: 22).

Spectacularising the tension between the particular will and the general will, *Mustang*'s affirmative aesthetics stands out among the emerging representations of youth and coming-of-age in contemporary cinema of Turkey. While *Mustang* invests in that tension and the ways in which its subject of coming-of-age resists the general will (of patriarchy and its imperative of marriage and kinship), the coming-of-age narratives in post-millennial Turkish cinema are dominated by the figure of the willful wanderer. Sara Ahmed notes that the willful wanderer 'stray[s] from the official pasts [...] create[s] desire lines, faint marks on the earth, as traces of where you or others have been' (2020: 21). Some of the willful subjects who dominate the youth films of Turkish cinema wander to remember a traumatic past or to reconcile with that trauma which requires the wanderer to wander away from the official paths of Turkish history (e.g. *Kaygı / Inflame* [2017], *Sonbahar / Autumn* [2018], *Gelecek Uzun Sürer / Future Lasts Forever* [2011], and *Tepenin Ardı / Beyond the Hill* [2012]). Others wander to find meaning through coming to terms with, and colliding against, parental and national authority (e.g. *Üç Maymun / Three Monkeys* [2008] and *The Wild Pear Tree* [2018]), and the uninhabitable general will it imposes (e.g. *Koca Dünya / Big Big World* [2016], *Jîn* [2013], *Hayat Var* (2008), and *Daha / More* [Saylak 2017]). There are also other willful subjects who wander, as strays, through the margins and peripheries due to their alienation from the hegemonic relations of gender, sexuality, class and/or ethnic identity (*Nefesim Kesilene Kadar / Until I Lose My Breath* [2015], *Şimdiki Zaman* [2012], *Koca Dünya* [2016], *Çoğunluk / Majority* [2010], *Kar / Snow* [2017], *Çekmeköy Underground* [2014], *Ferah Feza / Ships* [Refiğ 2013], *Başka Semtin Çocukları / Children of the Otherside* [2008], and *Kara Köpekler Havlarken / Black Dogs Barking* [2009]). Yet, conversely, the subject of coming-of-age in *Mustang* collides with power, and *wills* an escape, rather than embodying the alienated yet vulnerable position of the willful wanderer. Resonating with *2 Genç Kız* (2005) and *Arada / In Between* (2018), *Mustang*'s subject of girlhood is willing and willful: they assert their will to escape.[1]

There are various youth films produced in different national and international contexts, including *The Virgin Suicides*, *Girlhood*, and *Rocks*, which also frame their subjects of coming-of-age as a willful embodiment of collectivity and multiplicity. While most of these films pay particular attention to the narration of characters and the dramatisation of their relationships, *Mustang* refuses to psychologise the five sisters as individual characters with emotional interiority.

Working against the contemporary postfeminist representations of the 'tough girl' in popular cinema (e.g. the *Hunger Games* franchise) as a 'spectacularised and individualised embodiment of rebellion' (Smith 2020: 51; Shary 2014), *Mustang*'s 'five-headed monster' operates as an affirmative non-identitarian spectacle of joyful dissent. In this sense, the film's use of framing is very selective and thus expressive. While the joyful presence of *Mustang*'s 'five-headed creature' is prioritised on-screen, the grandmother's beating or the uncle's sexual abuse or the sisters' relationships with men (including their husbands) are never shown. Such selective framing in Ergüven's cinematography, leaving the pro-filmic events of violent and/or sexual exchange off-frame, serves the film's affirmative spectacle of willfulness. While the *mise-en-scène* and cinematography's function is to refuse an identitarian individualism and highlight the solidarity of the sisters (rather than their vulnerability and victimhood) by framing them in union as a joyful and dissident creature, the film's subject does not cohere around one particular will. *Mustang*'s five-headed body consists of willful parts with each part willing a different will in its encounter with the general will. When forced into marriage by her grandmother, Sonay, the oldest sister, protests her grandmother's choice and asserts her will to get married to her boyfriend Ekin. Convincing her grandmother, Sonay – as the willful subject – negotiates her particular will (i.e. her desire for Ekin) with the general will (i.e. the hetero-patriarchal imperative of marriage). Selma, however, does not resist at all when she is made to marry a boy she does not know at all. The willfulness in Selma's agreement, here, works as what Sara Ahmed defines as 'unwilling obedience':

> Thinking of willfulness as an embodied and shared vitality might help us to think of how willfulness is not always expressed as no. [...] [I]t is often more than obedience that is required by obedience (subjects must obey out of their own free will). It is thus possible that disobedience can take the form of an *unwilling obedience*: subjects might obey a command but do so grudgingly or reluctantly and enact with or through the compartment of their body a withdrawal from the right of the command even as they complete it.
> (2014: 140)

On her first night with her husband, Selma is taken to a hospital for a virginity test because the couple could not provide their family with the proof of Selma's virginity, i.e. the sheet with the blood of defloration. 'I slept with the entire world', Selma says to the doctor. When the doctor examines her and locates the intact hymen, Selma responds: 'I must have slept with someone and forgotten. Do you know how late it is? I'm very tired. When I say I'm a virgin, no one believes me. Why won't you leave me alone?' Here, Selma's unwilling surrender to the general will takes the form of a willful passivity.

While Selma's indifference and passivity is non-reactionary, Ece's indifference to her grandmother's mandate of marriage becomes reactionary and transgressive. 'When it was Ece's turn, at first she didn't react. Later she started behaving like she was looking for trouble', says Lale's voice-over. Having sex with a random guy in her uncle's car, and entertaining her sisters with obscene gestures to provoke her uncle, Ece collides with the general will of normative femininity through passive yet suicidal disobedience. Right after provoking her uncle to shout at her, Ece kills herself with his gun. Ece's suicide is the ultimate escape from the general will, which is also the ultimate compromise of willfulness, as the parental authority's 'punishment for willfulness is a passive willing of death, an allowing of death' (Ahmed 2014: 1). As Ahmed suggests, 'the will signifies that it is better to leave the right place than to stay in the right place because you are unable to move on your own' (12). If the general will's location of 'the right place' in *Mustang* is the marriage imposed upon the sisters, Ece shows her will to leave that place because she is 'unable to move on [her] own'.

The voice-over of Lale, the youngest sister, acts as the narrator throughout the film. Lale embodies not only the willful child of the five-headed creature but also the witness and the survivor in the film. Lale's point of view enables play, joy, and laughter to dominate the frame (rather than the burdens of identity politics); it also mobilises a departure from the dominant stylistic paradigms of social realism and poetic realism embedded in various contexts of world cinema, including the contemporary cinema of Turkey. Lale and Nur's escape from the family house is *Mustang*'s final willful act. Lale, the willful child who is plotting the escape throughout the film, allows the spectator to see the space through its locations of flight, rather than presenting it as a cage of immobility. Recalling Ahmed's conceptualisation of 'willfulness', we argue that the film treats Lale's will as a cinematic 'resource [...] bound up with a scene of overcoming' (Ahmed 2014: 37). Ahmed argues:

> The object of will is thus simultaneously an end: if to will is to will this or that, then willing has a particular end in sight, a realisation of a future possibility. We might describe the work of willing as accomplishment (to accomplish is to fulfil, fill up, complete). To will is to put one's energy into becoming accomplished in this way or that. This sense of will as *energetic*, as getting the body 'behind'

an action is important. It is not that the will is behind the subject but that willing might describe the feeling of getting behind something. If willing is an energetic relationship to a future possibility, not all possibilities become an object of will, not all possibilities require energy to become actualised. So I might will myself to write not only because I have an end in sight (becoming a writer, becoming one who has accomplished writing), but because I am blocked, or because I encounter myself as being blocked (the obstacle that gets in the way of the will can be myself and my own body). Willing might be *how* we encounter an obstacle as that which is to be overcome: we might perceive the will as a resource insofar as it is bound up with a scene of overcoming.

(ibid.)

What separates *Mustang* from most other coming-of-age stories in contemporary Turkish cinema is its investment in the sister's energetic will, and the ways in which the will 'encounter[s] and overcome[s] obstacle[s]'. The willful subjects of coming-of-age in post-millennial cinema of Turkey do not always act according to a particular 'end in sight', a 'realisation of a future possibility'. The wanderers of *Jîn*, *Koca Dünya*, *Hayat Var*, *Çoğunluk*, *Nefesim Kesilene Kadar*, and *Şimdiki Zaman* are willful yet not willing with a particular end (or a possibility of overcoming) in sight. However, each of *Mustang*'s willful sisters persists, in disobeying or unwillingly obeying, the general will. Lale, the willful child, is the only character willing and plotting an escape. Through the use of voice-over as the primary narrative tool, the film invites the viewer to identify with Lale's exit project, 'the object of [her] will' (38), that is, to escape, to stray, to defy from the general will, the heteropatriarchal imperative of marriage and its norms of femininity.

While Ergüven's selective framing spectacularises the sisters' willful mobility, it also stalls the narrative. On the one hand, *Mustang*'s diegetic tools can be considered to work through a narrative arc, where the collective will is gradually inhibited by the individualising forces of patriarchy and heteronormativity. On the other hand, the film's spectacularisation of joy and disobedience, intensified through its refusal to frame and dramatise oppression, abuse, and sex, contradicts the conventional diegesis of the coming-of-age genre. In her analysis of Sciamma's cinema, Smith argues that *Girlhood* effectively demonstrates Sciamma's subversive engagement with the conventions of the coming-of-age genre through her 'displacement of sexual experience from its pivotal spot in the American teen film' (2020: 21). Clara Bradbury-Rance's critical exploration of *Pariah* (Rees 2011) and its representation of queer adolescence asserts that Rees's film queers the coming-of-age films' generic 'expectation of an end point at which the protagonist has *come of age*', of an 'accomplishment of a movement', of an 'arrival': *Pariah* 'refuses to arrive' (2016: 90). As in *Pariah* and *Girlhood*, *Mustang*'s mobility does not depend on a diegetic resolution of sexual encounter or a redemptive accomplishment to 'come of age'. Decoupling the narrative from its generic function of arrival, accomplishment, assimilation, or redemption, *Mustang*'s diegetic progression is shaped by multiple vectors of flight.

Space: Nation, City/Province, Home

One of the key aesthetic components shaping the subject of coming-of-age in film is the on-screen space. Here, the cinematic space becomes an important formal element that helps one explore critically *where* the subject is located and *how* its body moves. Most coming-of-age films feature an intimate relationship between their protagonists and space. This spatial intimacy is also a dominant aesthetic paradigm in contemporary Turkish cinema that informs the diegetic world through the projective use of cityscapes, rural landscapes, and domestic interiors. *Mustang* evades this intimate relationship and presents the setting, *taşra* (the provinces) as an impersonal, non-projective space. Resonating with the point of view of the youngest sister Lale, whose voice-over drives the film's diegesis, Ergüven's *mise-en-scène* works as a performative refusal to grant *taşra*, and the domestic space, the power to immobilise the girls of *Mustang*, and obstruct their escape. Rather than trapping the girls within spaces regulated by norms, borders, and obstructions, the film's affirmative lens focuses on the lines of flight and mobility by inhibiting the allegorical power of *taşra* and home, and their dominant modes of representation in contemporary Turkish cinema.

'Provinciality', Asuman Suner argues, 'takes on differing meanings and is articulated through different visual modes' in what is usually canonised as the post-1990s 'New Cinema of Turkey' or 'New Turkish Cinema' (2002: 61). While a significant number of Turkish films belonging to this 'new wave' links provinciality to 'claustrophobia, spatial/social entrapment and circularity', the province in this trend can also 'become a peaceful site of contemplation and reconciliation with nature' (ibid.). Characterised by the *auteur* directors Zeki Demirkubuz and Nuri Bilge Ceylan, the dominant tropes of alienation, provinciality, and the city in 'New Turkish Cinema' are critiqued as significantly gendered, lumpen projections of estranged masculinity, where male characters often dominate the filmic space by operating as the willful wanderers of the city and the provinces (Akbal Süalp and Şenova 2008, Çakırlar and Güçlü 2013). This crisis in belonging is considered to also 'haunt' the representation of home as a 'prime site of the uncanny' (Suner 2004: 308). Re-appropriating spatial tropes of domesticity used in melodramas, the domestic interiors in these films become the spaces where the politics of gender, sexuality, ethnicity, and class unfolds through character relations (Suner 2004; Çakırlar and Güçlü 2013).

While the expressive use of the *mise-en-scène* maintains its key significance in post-millennial Turkish cinema, the dominant stylistic trends and the critical reach of gender/sexuality politics are more diverse than the earlier decades of filmmaking in Turkey. This diversity can also be observed in the recent proliferation of the coming-of-age films in Turkish cinema. Some of these films prioritise male youth and adolescence (*Çoğunluk / Majority* and *Koca Dünya*), while girls are also highly visible as protagonists of these youth and coming-of-age narratives in post-2000s filmmaking (e.g. *Sibel*, *Hayat Var*, *Nefesim Kesilene Kadar*, *Şimdiki Zaman*, and *Jîn*). These youth films also demonstrate a stylistic diversity; however, the range of stylistic innovation is still determined by various combinations of social realism, poetic realism, and documentary essayism (Akçalı 2019a, 2019b). In this sense, this dominance of realism in contemporary Turkish cinema echoes what Thomas Elsaesser also identifies as 'the *a priori* valorisation of realism in European cinema as the only valid ontology of the (photographic) image, based on its particular truth status of time (the indexicality of moment) and iconicity of place (what appears in the image corresponds to once-existing pro-filmic reality)' (2005: 487). 'The reliance on realism in European cinema', Elsaesser notes, 'go[es] hand in hand with a character psychology based on individual subjectivity, interiority, spiritual alienation, and social anomie – at the expense of fantasy, interpersonal conflict, action, and interactive communication as either "commercial" and low culture, or typical for Hollywood (action, spectacle)' (ibid.). *Mustang*'s evasion of the 'individual subjectivity' (through its five-headed embodiment of willful mobility) and its avoidance of the 'iconicity of place' (through its deconstruction of *taşra*) do indeed break away from an art-house realism that seems to dominate the representations of coming-of-age in Turkish and European cinemas. We will elaborate further on the extent to which Ergüven's choices of style and cinematography in *Mustang* stand out in comparison to other Turkish and European youth films. These formal choices, we contend, significantly inform the striking polarisation in the film's critical reception.

In her study on the emerging aesthetic patterns of post-millennial Turkish cinema, Övgü Gökçe pays particular attention to the ways in which landscape becomes a cinematographic tool to formulate alternative modes of articulating loss and political trauma (2009). Although youth does not constitute a distinct critical category of representation in Gökçe's study – a significant number of films that are part of the emerging aesthetic trends in Turkish cinema feature young protagonists. When speech and narrative fail to manifest the sentiment of loss, which becomes a burden for the young subject, inherited from the un-mourned losses of traumatic historical events, the filmic space becomes a site of exerting remembrance and mourning (Gökçe 2009: 278). The use of landscape in *Sonbahar* (2008) and *Gelecek Uzun Sürer* (2011), the performance of militarist masculinity in the allegorical war zone of *Tepenin Ardı* (2012), and the absence of the documentary records of the Madımak Massacre haunting the main character's perception of location in *Kaygı* (2017) are powerful examples of the ways in which the representation of space unsettles hegemonic scripts of national identity, triggers political traumas, and enables the young characters to remember and come to terms with them. Furthermore, rural landscapes are also often depicted as spaces that accommodate and reflect the dramas of childhood and adolescence through the lens of poetic realism. The children of *Beş Vakit / Times and Winds* (Erdem 2006), *Sivas* (2014), *Kuzu / The Lamb* (Ataman 2014), *Zefir* (2010), and *Bal / Honey* (Kaplanoğlu 2010) are depicted as willful wanderers of the rural landscape, whose rites of passage are either associated with myths of nature (*Beş Vakit*, *Zefir*, and *Bal*) or presented as a process of negotiation with gender norms (*Sivas* and *Kuzu*). The female protagonists of *Jîn* (2013) and *Kız Kardeşler / A Tale of Three Sisters* (2019), however, are representations of coming-of-age where the subject does not dissolve in an ideologically overdetermining rural/natural landscape but asserts her mobility (*Jîn*) and relationality (*Kız Kardeşler*).

'Contemporary Turkish cinema', Aytaç and Onaran argue, 'reveals particular tendencies in the depiction of *taşra*' whereas it manifests the urban space, especially Istanbul, 'as an elusive and vast space/place that can be comprehended only in pieces and fragments' (2007: 22). The characters of the post-millennial youth films are willful wanderers who experience the city 'in pieces and fragments'. The city becomes a stifling place, a site of corruption, segregation, and regeneration, in which the protagonists are trapped and want to escape from. Yet, the mobilities of these characters are considerably limited due to economic precarity and/or ethnic marginalisation. Mina's aspirations to move to the USA in *Şimdiki Zaman* (2012), Serap's persistence in surviving abuse and financial precarity in *Nefesim Kesilene Kadar* (2015), the complex drama of the hip-hop youth in Istanbul's suburbs in *Çekmeköy Underground* (2015), the entrapment of the young members of Istanbul's segregated Alevi community in *Başka Semtin Çocukları* (2008), and the dystopic vision of Istanbul and its young residents in *Hayaletler* (2020) are only a few examples that demonstrate fragmented visions of the city, and the identity crises experienced within its 'pieces and fragments', defining the aesthetic and critical universe of contemporary Turkish cinema. The majority of these films feature a dissident, willful youth, who are rooted in, yet estranged from, the city they reside in.

In her in-depth analysis of Sciamma's *Girlhood* (2014), Frances Smith argues that the film 'feminis[es] the *banlieue*' (2020: 31) by intervening into its construction as a 'largely masculine-defined space' in French cinema. Contrasting Sciamma's use of setting in *Girlhood* with Kassovitz's vision of the *banlieue* in *La Haine* (1995), Smith suggests that Sciamma reverses the gendered associations of mobility with the *banlieue* by 'present[ing] young women as embodiments of mobility' and male characters as 'rooted in the exterior landscapes of the banlieue' (37). Smith also suggests that Sciamma's earlier work (e.g. *Naissance des Pieuvres / Water Lillies* [2007] and *Tomboy* [2011]) treats space as 'deliberately blank and largely lacking in signifiers of Frenchness so as to foreground the seduction and brutality of [character relations]' (40–1). Sciamma's cinematic engagement with space resonates with Ergüven's deliberate anonymisation of space (that is, the Turkish province) to foreground the affirmative mobility of the film's gendered subject rather than reproducing the allegorical affiliations of *taşra* and its weight on character relations.

The village where the story of *Mustang* takes place is presented as a considerably non-descript place. The province is not named, and the obscure accents of the film's characters do not reveal any regional specificity. The reference to a football match (with the team Trabzonspor playing) and a dialogue referring to the village being '1000 kilometres away from Istanbul' implies that the story is taking place in a small and remote village by the Turkish Black Sea coast (in northern/northeastern Turkey). The film opens with the sisters' last day at school and we see a number of students heading to the coast and playing in the sea in their school uniforms. The association of sea (or ocean) with youthfulness is a globally established motif that can also be observed in various Turkish coming-of-age films (e.g. *Mavi Dalga, Ferah Feza, Daha,* and *Geçen Yaz / Last Summer* [Açıktan 2021]). This opening scene also functions as a juxtaposition of the collective joy of youth with what awaits the sisters soon after, that is, the individualising and oppressing forces of the conservative family obsessed with controlling the willful excess of youth with patriarchal imperatives of chastity, marriage, and honour. Yet, this juxtaposition does not necessarily lead to representations of spaces and settings as cages of imprisonment that limit the sisters' mobility entirely. They are in constant movement even when they are grounded at home. Resonating with the film's deliberately impersonal non-descript village, Ergüven's cinematography here assumes a distinct optic that prioritises spaces of flight and mobility rather than those of entrapment and immobility. In the first half of the film, we see the sisters are plotting multiple escapes, including Sonay's nightly escapes from her room's window to meet her boyfriend Ekin, and the sisters' escape from the house to see a football match at a stadium. Rather than presenting the viewer with a poetic and dramatic account of the Turkish provincial life that is supposed to contextualise the introspective depth of the characters, Ergüven refuses to allegorise *taşra* and focuses instead on its borders while they are crossed by the sisters in various ways. What dominate *Mustang*'s filmic space are fences, windows, garden borders, and the highway road which connects the film's non-descriptive village to other Turkish towns and cities (see Figure 2.2). Echoing Smith's reading of Sciamma and her engagement with the *banlieue*, *Mustang*'s male characters do not embody a privileged mobility (except Yasin, the young male driver the sisters come across during their escape to the football match, who later becomes friends with Lale and teaches her how to drive), while the mobility of women shapes the film's cinematography and diegesis.

Ergüven's affirmative optic, prioritising the girls' willful mobility rather than their vulnerability and victimhood, can also be observed in the film's representation of domestic interiors. While the family house is where the sisters are grounded by their grandmother, the film avoids a pathos of immobility or entrapment and focuses on the zones of flight within the domestic space. Although the house is presented as a patriarchal apparatus, a space of familial control, and a place of punitive training, Ergüven does not frame it as a stifling dwelling but juxtaposes its status as a repressive container with its points of flight: windows, doors, and the garden (particularly its borders). This affirmative account of space in the film refuses to internalise a gritty cinematic realism of gender violence, and makes the *mise-en-scène* project the sisters' point of view. As mentioned, Sonay escapes the house through its windows several times at night to meet her boyfriend Ekin. The sisters plot another escape to go to a football match in a nearby city. While the grandmother builds more fences around the house to avoid any more escape plans,

Figure 2.2 Spaces of flight in *Mustang*.

the film does not interrupt the sisters' joyful presence in the house. They laugh. They play games. They sunbathe in swimsuits against the fences. Ergüven appropriates the filmic status of the domestic space as a melodramatic trope to register the protagonists' willful mobility by de-dramatising the domestic entrapment and replacing it with an affirmative excess of joy (see Figures 2.3 and 2.4).

We argue that the majority of both Euro-American and Turkish reviews fail to fully capture the potential of Ergüven's affirmative use of space. While most Anglophone and Francophone critics reduce the film's representational framework to a spectacle of empowerment

56 *Framing the Willful Subject*

Figure 2.3 Windows as melodramatic trope in *Mustang*.

by overinterpreting the Turkish political context with no nuance, and imposing an oppressor/oppressed and victim/survivor dialectic, most Turkish reviews quickly judge the film's stylistic register of realism and question the authenticity of its representation of various spatial affiliations, including nation, city/province, and home. Echoing Ceuterick's reading of *Wadjda* and its representation of space, Ergüven's use of locations and settings 'produce[s] micro-instances of affirmation, drawing lines of flight that points toward what is not yet there' (2020: 119).

While most of the 'Turkish' films incorporated into our comparative framework so far were supported by European funders for

Framing the Willful Subject 57

Figure 2.4 House as cage in *Mustang*.

their production and international distribution, Çağla Zencirci and Guillaume Giovanetti's film *Sibel* (2018), another European (Turkey-France-Germany-Luxembourg) co-production, can be considered as *Mustang*'s 'sister film' in terms of its interstitial, collaborative, cross-cultural authorship. Both films adopt an affirmative optic that presents the subject of coming-of-age as willful, and locate the protagonists in a positively obscured setting of *taşra*. *Sibel*'s lead character is a young woman, Sibel, who lives with her father and sister in a secluded village of the Black Sea region. She is mute and communicates only by using the ancestral whistle language of the region. Marginalised by her fellow villagers, she hunts wolves and collects bones in the forest, and comes across a fugitive, a man who has escaped from his mandatory military service. Through the amorous relationship between these two characters, the film explores Sibel's sexual awakening, which facilitates a critique of tradition and its patriarchal gender politics. However, unlike *Mustang*, *Sibel*'s treatment of space does not evade an allegorical urge. Sibel's muteness, or her refusal to speak the official language of Turkey, produces a gendered outcast falling outside the norms of patriarchy and ethnonationalism. The film treats the forest as a place of wildness that contains not only Sibel's transgressive desire for the fugitive man but also the bones of the adversary 'creatures', which Sibel will realise to be human remains rather than the wolves she protects the village against. In contrast to *Mustang*'s refusal to represent *taşra*, *Sibel* locates Sibel's willfulness within an allegory of national politics.

Both *Sibel* and *Mustang* present a rural community whose patriarchal norms are consolidated by women through a surveillance culture embedded in village life. The willful protagonists of both films contest these women who act as gatekeepers of patriarchy. However, the representation of, and the friction between, the individual and collective will, differs considerably in these films. *Mustang*'s framing of the sisters as a 'five-headed monster' facilitates an affirmative aesthetic of a collective will that resists the individualising forces of patriarchy whereas *Sibel* individualises its subject. The narrative progression of Sibel's 'coming-of-age' mobilises a relationality that re-organises relations among young women in the village by extending Sibel's individual will to a collective 'will-to-come'. *Mustang*'s narrative, however, dramatises the resilience of the sisters' collective will to defy the patriarchal norms and to escape their domestic confinement.

The Maternal Closet

From the earlier productions of the Yeşilçam era (1950s–1970s) appropriating established tropes of melodrama, to the *arabesk* films (1970s–1980s) featuring child stars, popular Turkish cinema has been shaped significantly by dramas of parenthood. Fatherhood and motherhood in these films work through a gendered discourse that produces 'bad'/corrupt and 'good'/devoted parents. The alternative filmmaking in the 1990s, often defined as 'New Turkish Cinema', contested these normative dichotomies. Prioritising male-centred narratives, these filmmaking practices capitalised upon a crisis in masculinity (Akbal Süalp and Şenova 2008; Suner 2010). This crisis was often projected onto insecure father figures while women, especially mothers, were frequently invisible in these films' critical interventions into the normative constructions of family and parenthood. What has emerged in post-millennial filmmaking practices, however, is a more nuanced approach that integrates the critical depictions of motherhood into the stories in which the insecure fathers still persist (e.g. *Daha* [2017], *Hayat Var* [2008], *Üç Maymun* [2008], and *Çoğunluk* [2010]). We contend that this emergence of maternal characters in Turkish cinema is also informed by the integration of women directors into the national film sector.

The representations of motherhood in post-millennial Turkish cinema complicate the 'good vs. bad' oppositions and intervene in the moralising frameworks which dominated the cinematic heritage of Yeşilçam and *arabesk* films. The cultural imaginary of sacralised motherhood is replaced with more complex and diverse maternal characters. The manipulative symbiotic mother–daughter relationships in *Ana Yurdu* (2015) and *Köksüz* (2013), the transgressive mothers involved in extramarital affairs in *Süt / Milk* (Kaplanoğlu 2008) and *Üç Maymun* (2008), neglectful or avoidant mothers in *Çoğunluk* (2010), *2 Genç Kız* (2005), and *Zefir* (2010), protective yet oppressive mothers in *Kuzu* (2014), *Ahlat Ağacı* (2018), *Tamam Mıyız? / Are We Okay?* (Irmak 2013) and *Zenne* (2010), are only a few examples of films granting their maternal characters a complex interiority that goes beyond the 'good vs. bad' and 'dissident vs. hegemonic' binaries. While these mothers are more relational, powerful, and textured characters when compared with the more heteronormative tropes of maternity embedded in Turkey's cinematic heritage, most of these films critically engage with the maternal will which negotiates, if not entirely re-consolidates, the patriarchal oppression in different ways. Denying the maternal characters the unquestionable virtue of devotion and selfless care, some of these postmillennial films also expose the mothers' complicity in their children's (and their own) oppression.

The grandmother in *Mustang* resonates with this emerging maternal subject of Turkish cinema. Performing the role of the maternal guardian who protects the family honour and her orphaned granddaughters' chastity, *Mustang*'s grandmother embodies the oppressive force of patriarchy and its gendered mandates of virginity and marriage. Yet the film exposes the hypocrisy of her protective care: she imprisons her granddaughters, forces them into arranged marriages, and ignores her son's sexual abuse of Nur. The film's treatment of the grandmother as the 'gatekeeper' of patriarchy also makes the domestic space work as a Sedgwickian closet: containing the subject of coming-of-age by immobilising her body and controlling her sexuality, the grandmother's house in the film works as a maternal closet that simultaneously acknowledges and polices the girls' willfulness, including their sexuality (see Figure 2.5). While the filmic space is treated as a 'glass closet', that is, the closet of an 'open secret' (Sedgwick 1990: 165), *Mustang*'s subject of girlhood refuses to be contained and regulated by it.

In this regard, the grandmother's wardrobe has an important metonymic function in the film. Embodying the maternal will to contain the girls' collective will, the wardrobe literalises the spatial function of the house as a filmic metaphor of the closet. Ergüven pays particular attention to what the wardrobe contains throughout the film. The girls' belongings locked in the wardrobe, away from their reach, include

60 *Framing the Willful Subject*

Figure 2.5 Grandmother's house in *Mustang*.

Figure 2.6 Delacroix's *Liberty* in *Mustang*.

telephones, smartphones, computers, colourful clothes, make-up kits, a t-shirt with a #DirenGezi print, a small reproduction of Delacroix's *Liberty Leading the People* (1830), and a book titled *Cinsel Hayatım* (*My Sexual Life*) (see Figures 2.6 and 2.7). Symbolising the girls' oppressed agency, these sequestered items reflect Ergüven's discourse of transnational feminism by locating her authorship against the hegemonic national politics of post-secular neoliberal conservatism in Turkey. While the co-existence of the #DirenGezi t-shirt and the smartphones associates the film's subject of coming-of-age with an emergent transnational culture of youth and dissent (e.g. the political mobilisations of youth through the social media such as the #Occupy movement), the reference to Delacroix's *Liberty* (idealising freedom as feminine) reflects

Framing the Willful Subject 61

Figure 2.7 The maternal closet and the Gezi t-shirt in *Mustang*.

Ergüven's refusal to ground the girls' will within a national cinema's defeatist register of introspective realism. Inserting Delacroix's setting of the French Revolution to an iconic setting of Turkish cinema (i.e. *taşra*), does not only demonstrate Ergüven's interstitial authorial position at the margins of Turkish and French national cinemas but also encapsulate the divisions of the film's critical reception and its failure to fully capture Ergüven's articulation of resistance and willfulness beyond national ideologies and belonging. This is discussed in more detail in Chapter 3.

Ranging from the fences and windows of the grandmother's house to the remoteness of its provincial location, Ergüven's affirmative use of the *mise-en-scène* highlights borders as immobilising forces while celebrating the sisters' willful agency and resilient determination to transgress these borders multiple times throughout the film. Similarly, the representation of sex and sexuality focuses on transgression rather than oppression, although it avoids spectacularisation of sexual relations. The girls' virginity is treated as the ultimate evidence of their chastity and they are subjected to virginity tests to reassure the families. Yet, the hypocritical obsession with the hymen is juxtaposed with Ergüven's representation of the sisters as actively desiring, sexual subjects. Sonay tells Selma that she has already started having sex with her boyfriend Ekin and they have anal sex to avoid breaking Sonay's hymen. As part of her vengeful self-destruction before she commits suicide, Ece has sex with a random boy in her uncle's car. Through this sexual excess, the film treats the hymen as an artificial border that does not necessarily obstruct the girls' sexual desire.

However, the sexual relations are not spectacularised as a conventional rite of passage. In her reading of *Naissance des Pieuvres / Water Lilies*, Frances Smith notes that Sciamma's film 'banalises' the loss of virginity by representing it in an 'undramatic way' (2020: 18). Emma Wilson reads Sciamma's treatment of the hymen in *Naissance* as a subversive strategy to 're-make a coming-of-age film' whose characters embrace pain in willfully breaking the 'membrane ... between childhood and adulthood' (2021: 37). While *Mustang*'s representation of hymen-as-concept (or hymen-as-border) resonates with Sciamma's urge to banalise defloration and subvert the cultural norms surrounding the hymen, Ergüven also carries out a critique of its cultural weaponisation by unsettling its normative function to symbolise chastity and innocence. Chastity loses its symbolic function through the protagonists' multiple exposures to sex throughout the film. Besides Ece's self-destructive sexual encounter in public and Sonay's confession of anal intercourse, Selma's hymen does not break following her first night with her husband, which raises doubts about her virginity. Insistently taking the girls to the hospital for virginity tests, the uncle continues raping Nur at night.

Informed by Ergüven's affirmative gaze prioritising lines of flight rather than spaces of arrest or immobility, *Mustang*'s conceptual treatment of the hymen resonates with the film's engagement with other spatial borders which are crossed multiple times, including those of the province, the house (i.e. fences and windows), and the grandmother's wardrobe. Sarah Ahmed asserts that 'to become willfully estranged from femininity is to become a stranger to the family' (2014: 90). *Mustang*'s girls become willfully estranged from the moral framework of de-sexualised femininity and its obsession with virginity/hymen. Staging the girls' affective excess, including sexual desire, the film makes them strangers to family. Their persistence while trapped in the cage of the maternal closet (i.e. a closet that comes to existence through the grandmother's internalisation of patriarchal values) antagonises 'family values'. Perhaps, the girls' affective excess subverts the reduction of femininity's moral purity into the hymen. Even with an intact hymen, none of *Mustang*'s girls are 'virgin enough' as they refuse to enact the general will of femininity by insisting on their particular will. Chastity, as it is culturally imposed, becomes an uninhabitable position for *Mustang*'s girls – even with intact hymens. If patriarchy subordinates the subject to its reproductive mandate, which, Ahmed asserts, 'requires the evacuation of desire from will' (Ahmed 2014: 120), *Mustang* treats the hymen as an unwilling yet willful object. Such an object does not allow desire to be evacuated from the general will's sacralisation of hymen and its celebration of marriage through its breaking. The book *Cinsel Hayatım / My Sexual Life*, which the grandmother keeps in her wardrobe and takes out each time a granddaughter is to get married, represents the maternal will's attempt to collapse the girls' sexuality into the general will of patriarchal marriage and its mandate of chastity. *Mustang*'s girls escape the maternal closet as they cross all other artificially policed borders in the film.

Affirmative chromo-politics

In his analysis of Sofia Coppola's *The Virgin Suicides* (1999), Justin Wyatt argues that the film's appropriation of melodrama contains moments of stylistic excess that 'break the diegetic world, creating a space for joy and happiness for the characters' (2019: 66). Considering these moments of excess as 'visual bursts', Wyatt also sees them as Coppola's pastiche of the 1970s' advertising aesthetic in the US, and the controversies around the sexualisation of youth and children (73–4). While *Mustang* and *The Virgin Suicides* may be seen to share an affirmative aesthetic in their strategic engagement with melodrama and its gendered tropes, the meanings embedded in *Mustang*'s implementation of 'visual bursts' differ from those informed by Coppola's 'indie' aesthetic of re-appropriation. Ergüven's use of colour is a key component of *Mustang*'s expressive *mise-en-scène*. While pink and red assert and affirm the libidinal excess of coming-of-age (informing the girls' agency and willfulness), brown signifies bodily oppression and domestic confinement.

Apart from a limited number of films with 'visual bursts', including Kutluğ Ataman's *2 Genç Kız* (2005) and Reha Erdem's *Hayat Var* (2008), the subjects of youth or coming-of-age in the post-millennial Turkish cinema are often dramatised through the chromo-normative cinematography of realisms. The *chiaroscuro* effects of Nuri Bilge Ceylan's films (such as *Üç Maymun*), and the gritty colour palettes articulating class precarity in *Nefesim Kesilene Kadar* (2015), *Ferah Feza* (2013), and *Daha* (2017) treat colour as the marker of oppression, introspection, and vulnerability, which operate as an antagonising effect in relation to the characters' agency. In this regard, *Mustang*'s use of colour intervenes in the chromo-normativity of realist cinema and its dominant associations with world cinema.

The pink colour is used throughout the film to register the reactive excess of Lale as the willful child. She wears her sister's pink bra and performs a catwalk in the house. She hoovers the house in a pink pair of socks, and uses a pink fly swatter to kill the flies in the house. She plays with a pink ball by hitting it against the cement walls of the house yard. A pink pompom pen is used when Lale studies her coursebook on 'citizenship rights'. Using gender-normative connotations of the pink colour while conflating femininity, sexuality, play, and action with childhood, *Mustang*'s use of pink functions to assert not only Lale's agency as a character but also the film's diegetic positioning of her as the narrator.

Similarly, the red colour works as the 'visual burst' of desire in the film. Following the grandmother's punishment of grounding the girls, Sonay's boyfriend Ekin paints his declaration of his love ('Benimsin Sonay' meaning 'You're Mine Sonay') onto the entrance road in front of the house. Lale's friendship with Yasin, the only male 'ally' in the film, helps the film communicate Lale's commitment to escape in an expressive manner. Asking Yasin to teach her how to drive, Lale wears her red shoes for her driving tutorial. The red colour here does not only signify Lale's desire to escape but also imply her desire for Yasin (see Figure 2.8).

Ranging from the clothes locked in the grandmother's closet, and the swimsuits the girls wear in the house, to the colours of celebration at the

Figure 2.8 The politics of pink and red in *Mustang*.

Framing the Willful Subject 65

Figure 2.9 'Shit-coloured' dresses in *Mustang*.

football match the girls go to (without permission), the bright colours surround the girls' bodies throughout the film. These 'visual bursts' are juxtaposed with what Lale deems as the 'shit colour'. Ergüven treats the colour brown as the colour of 'modesty' antagonising the willful energy of the girls' supplements by the 'bursts' of pink and red. Confronting Petek Hanım and protesting her misleading scrutinisation of the girls' play with boys as immoral (leading to the girls' punishment by their grandmother), Lale asks: 'Do your shapeless shit-coloured clothes make you everyone's moral judge?' The 'shapeless shit-coloured clothes' in the film signify women's self-surveillance and moral gatekeeping. As part of the grandmother's punitive scheme, the girls are forced to wear baggy, brown-coloured dresses that cover their bodies. Brown, then, is treated as the colour of the patriarchal self-policing of women. This further resonates with the wooden brown colour of the house exteriors and the grandmother's wardrobe, that is, spatial tropes of the closet demonstrating maternal complicity in oppressing the willful child and youth (see Figure 2.9).

Palatable Foreignness and the Limits of Intelligibility

This chapter focused on the ways in which *Mustang*'s 'mid brow' transnational style informs its representation of gender, dissent, and coming-of-age. Ergüven's expressive use of *mise-en-scène* and cinematography constructs a globally palatable filmic space to depict gender-based violence and resistance. The film's stylistic register, which seems to evade the New Turkish Cinema's realist investment in spatial tropes and national allegory, and privileges an affirmative aesthetic of willful dissent, facilitates a transnational feminist optic. However, Ergüven's transnational (and in her own words, 'universal[ising]') approach to the representation of youth and coming-of-age also exposes geopolitically marked limits of the film's national and transnational intelligibility. While most interlocutors of Turkish critical reception question the film's authenticity and verisimilitude in contesting the film's (and Ergüven's) obscure national affiliations, the international (especially Francophone and Anglophone) critical reception celebrates the film's representation of empowered girlhood by (mis-)interpreting it through a humanitarian spectacle of vulnerability and oppression. Although *Mustang*'s affirmative aesthetics constructs a transnational subject of coming-of-age, the film's interstitial location at the categorical margins of 'national cinema' and 'world cinema' provokes divergent, and geopolitically situated, critical standpoints. What these critiques share, though, is an attempt to objectify willful girlhood by reducing it into its national affiliations and thus obscuring the agency and the affirmative force of its willful subject of coming-of-age. As will become clearer in Chapter 3, *Mustang* is a powerful example of transnational filmmaking practice, which runs the risk of being located within film criticism's dominant discourses of identity politics despite the filmmaker's stylistic attempts to evade national belonging and to affirm willful agency.

Note

1 The will to escape is an important trope in the post-millennial youth films of Turkish cinema. The willful characters of the films *Hayat Var* (2008), *Jin* (2013), and *Şimdiki Zaman* (2013) are also plotting an escape and assert their desires for mobility.

3 Critical Reception
Paradoxes of National Belonging and Geopolitics of Film Criticism

'As a metaphor for Turkish schizophrenia, torn between patriarchy and modernity, this stylised fable, which spins like a galloping horse, will undoubtedly appeal to a Western audience', writes Isabelle Regnier in a review published in *Le Monde* (Regnier 2015) soon after *Mustang* was screened in Cannes. A year later, when the film was nominated by France for Best Foreign Language Film at the Oscars, 'French filmmakers took offence', according to another review in *Libération* (Diatkine 2016), which explains the efforts of Charles Gillibert, the film's producer, to ease the French film industry's hostility towards the choice. Disapproving this position and in favour of the film's Frenchness, Diatkine notes: 'This is to forget that the nationality of a film is determined by its production. And that the filmmaker, trained in a French film school, owes everything to France. And that *Mustang*, which shows the desire for freedom of five young girls struggling with patriarchy and a stifling religiosity, defends truly French values' (ibid.). For many critics from Turkey, the film's 'appeal to a Western audience' and 'defence for truly French values' is equally obvious, supported by the claim that its style and narrative fulfil a desire to lay bare a sharp split 'between patriarchy and modernity', inscribed in the film as a dichotomy of traditionalism and secularism as perceived from a superior and foreign viewpoint. Most agree that the film 'carries marks of mainstream French culture' (Özakın 2015), and it is this quality of being 'designed for the Western world in a meticulously calculated way [that makes] *Mustang* [...] a disturbingly orientalist work' (Ercivan 2015).

Although the critical interpretations of the film are varied in tone and position, validating and defining this 'appeal' (Regnier 2015), whether as the result of a 'West European sensibility' (Weissberg 2015) or a 'colonised gaze' (Saygılı 2016), is a fundamental drive that shapes the language of criticism. The film's highly stylised art-house look paired

DOI: 10.4324/9781003089056-4

with a contemporary story taking place in a village in Turkey makes it an odd example amongst similar productions from Turkey in global circulation. Arguably, this oddity is a common theme for most critics; the challenge of defining and classifying it sets up their evaluative criteria. In internationally acclaimed films such as *Kış Uykusu / Winter Sleep* (Ceylan 2015), *Bal / Honey* (Kaplanoğlu 2010) and *Pandoranın Kutusu / Pandora's Box* (Ustaoğlu 2008), filmmakers have assumed or rather appropriated realism as a distinguishing stylistic approach complementing rural narratives; *Mustang*'s diversion from these films, especially in terms of its global art-house look, challenges expectations. *Mustang* neither follows the common realistic mode of address nor treats its characters as victims produced by oppressive societies. The film's narrative is driven by stylistic excess that spectacularises willful girlhood. In this respect, the film does not look 'Turkish'; and the fact that its filmmaker is 'Turkish-French' makes matters more complicated. The influence of Ergüven's identity on the film's style shapes most of the topics in critical discussions, ranging from an emphasis on the lack of specificities in the setting to an exposed and aestheticised portrayal of female coming-of-age. This is a transnational film, or what Naficy (1999) calls 'interstitial' in terms of its production, distribution, and exhibition modes; however, its style and subject matter challenge the established tropes of exilic, migrant, or accented style. Nevertheless, having been made by a director born in Turkey, and with international funding, its transnationality is a matter to be debated in the reviews, often affecting value judgements. Ergüven is marked as an outsider or an insider to Turkey according to the discursive stance that the critic takes. The ambivalence around the difficulty of identifying *Mustang* as (trans)national pertains to the filmmaker's 'migrant-by-choice' identity. Ergüven was not forced into exile, she is a privileged migrant coming from an upper middle-class family who travelled mainly between France and Turkey due to her father's diplomatic duty and finally chose to settle in France as a teenager. These are details brought up both in her interviews and the film's reviews demonstrating how critics have problematised the liminality of her national identity, which they have used in their evaluating criteria to scrutinise or celebrate a variety of elements of style and subject in *Mustang*. The film's reception becomes an exercise in translating how this uncategorised transnational identity has been inscribed in the film's narration and narrative, shaped by each critic's own discursive positioning towards women, youth, nationalism, secularism and conservatism in Turkey and beyond.

This chapter offers a comparative examination of *Mustang*'s reception via analyses of film reviews and critical articles published in Turkish,

French, and English. The style and content of the language of criticism effectively demonstrates the ways in which diverse institutions of criticism perceive economic, social, and cultural boundaries of national and transnational cinema, evident in the critics' applied criteria for filmic evaluation. Recognising *Mustang* is seemingly a task of interpreting its cinematic qualities by locating it in a nation's film culture and assessing its strengths and weaknesses through a filter of what Turkish, French, or Turkish-French means. This practice also demonstrates the gendered, normative, and nation-bound idiosyncrasies of criticism as an ideological institution.

In *Scattered Hegemonies*, Kaplan works with 'politics of location', a term first introduced by Adrienne Rich to critique the universalising aspect of Western feminism that ignores differences arising from imbalanced and diverse power relationships within different cultures (Kaplan 1994). This term can be utilised in the discussions of *Mustang*'s critical reception. Kaplan argues that 'post-modern theories that link subject positions to geographical and metaphorical locations have emerged out of a perception that periodisation and linear historical forms of explanation have been unable to account fully for the production of complex identities in an era of diaspora and displacement' and adds that 'we need critical practices that mediate the most obvious oppositions, interrogating the terms that mythologise our differences and similarities' (138). In line with this proposition, our aim is to demonstrate the obvious viewpoints of criticism from Turkey, France, and elsewhere, and offer a depiction of how the film becomes legible to different tastes and desires informed by nationalist, orientalist, or sexist discourses. Moreover, we suggest an alternative reading of the film, as laid out in the previous chapters, which is less satiated with politics of representation within the diegesis but reveals the significance of the film in terms of its uniqueness in engagement with gender politics in Turkey and expressiveness of female agency and coming-of-age. We contend that such a reading transcends matters of geographical positioning and ownership in local and global reception via how girlhood, familial oppression, and rural life in Turkey are represented in the film, and allows for a more eclectic comprehension of contemporary transnational filmmaking than that offered in reviews.

Style and Verisimilitude

As Kaplan writes, 'recognizing the limits of a politics of location does not obviate the need for terms and concepts that help us address the tensions between conventional oppositions such as global/local and

West/non-West' (1994: 148). Since our work contextualises and analyses *Mustang* amongst a growing number of contemporary coming-of-age films from Turkey, we find it appropriate to refer to criticism published in Turkey as 'local', and the rest as 'global', being mindful of the common topics covered within those reviews published in France. *Mustang* got immediate international attention at its Cannes premiere in May 2015. While the reviews in French and English peaked in May – and in the following months with the film's release throughout Europe – it got limited press coverage in Turkey until October, when it was shown in a festival, *Film Ekimi*, in Istanbul and later got its theatrical release in Turkey. The announcement of *Mustang*'s nomination for Oscars by France in late 2015 stirred the critical spheres once more about the film's 'identity' and 'belonging'.[1] The coverage that we look at contains articles, reviews, and interviews in popular journals, newspapers, and magazines, online and in print, spanning the period that starts from the time of the film's first theatrical screening in Cannes in May 2015 until after the Oscar ceremony in late February 2016 when the film was released for a second time in Turkey. The recurring themes and ideas in this selection of media coverage published in three languages, French, English, and Turkish, are varied in their focus, tone, and interpretation, offering a distinctive example through which to discuss the richness of possible meanings stemming from a single work. Yet what strikes us in this variety of responses is how subject matters such as femininity, youth, sexuality, and oppression – *Mustang*'s main themes – are addressed from discrete ideologically informed critical positions, and how these positions reflect the assumed 'local' and 'global' viewpoints in owning and differentiating cultural products as well as societies and nations.

As discussed in Chapter 2, *Mustang*'s style, in contrast to a significant number of willful characters in Turkish coming-of-age films, works to spectacularise willfulness in various forms, including those of disobedience, desire, escape, or passive volition. This stylistic excess, we argue, is one of *Mustang*'s core features that leads to the film's polarised critical reception. Whether coming from a local or a global critic, this excess is recognised as an oddity amongst other *taşra*-themed cinema and female coming-of-age films from Turkey, and it is one of the film's qualities that the critics struggle to categorise and interpret. What seems to be the most popular point of entry into the film's critical reception is the portrayal of young girls as willful subjects of dissent, and the juxtaposition of their highly vocal, sexually active, protesting, and resisting presence with the rural setting. It is this portrayal that is frequently interpreted as an 'orientalist', 'universal', 'foreign', 'unrealistic', or 'feminist' look to growing up in rural Turkey in both negative and positive terms. One reviewer from Turkey criticises 'the extra significance ascribed to the girls' sexualities' (Özakın 2015). She finds the title stereotypical as the female body is equated with a wild horse: 'instead of providing each girl's dreams, differences in personality traits, or interests, the film focuses on the energy in their bodies via this metaphor in the title' (ibid.). She argues that the camera has a voyeuristic look and that 'the male gaze, which approaches the female body in an attempt to exploit and consume it, is reproduced through the eyes of a female director' (ibid.).

Indeed, equating female energy on screen with voyeurism is assuming the position of the audience as male-only, but it appears that the critical reception in Turkey focused more on seeing sexually commodified girls rather than liberated and feminised girlhood. Perhaps it is Ergüven's expressive stylistic choices in framing, lighting, and composition that trigger reviewers to use the word 'eroticism' (Bötke 2015; Daldal 2015; Şen 2015; Alibeygil 2016) when writing about the film's depiction of the girls. Apparently, the way the girls visually occupy the frame with their bodies and lead the narrative with a series of events centred on their subjectivity is not identified as part of a feminist aesthetics; instead, it is recognised as a misrepresentation of female sexuality and oppression of women in Turkey 'packaged' for a Western audience. For one reviewer, for instance, the play between boys and girls in the sea in their school uniforms at the start of the film is alienating: 'one wonders', he writes, 'whether young girls living in İnebolu, Kastamonu, having such comfort about their bodies is realistic' (Ercivan 2015). According to another critic, girls would not behave as such because 'especially in Anatolia, boys are taught violence and girls are taught the importance of being decent at an early age' (Bötke 2015). The film is even accused of 'not focusing on women's issues, but because of its incorrect editing/narrativizing, it exploits women's issues and profits from them' (Saygılı 2016).

The reviews rarely attend to the filmic narration: rather than focusing on the ways in which the filmmaker has chosen to tell the story, offering certain viewing positions to follow it – such as the strategic choice of the voice-over to match the youngest sister Lale's point of view with the film's stylistic excess – most attention is directed at narrative and representation. The figure of the teenage girl is analysed via terms as enunciated by ideological discourses, be it nationalism, orientalism, or sexism. It is interesting that many reviewers neglect to mention the fact that child marriages, endogamy, incest, virginity tests, and sexual violence against women are not uncommon in Turkey.[2] At a time when a woman's right to wear shorts is disputed,[3] it could easily be claimed that both in reality and on screen, the female body is expected to be enclosed

72 *Critical Reception*

and confined in contemporary Turkey. *Mustang*'s girls are not validated or defined by boys or by any relationship they pursue with patriarchy. They only rely on one another, they are loud, clear, and opinionated, and they are never shown to seek approval from anyone. Seemingly, the girls' resistance against being victimised by an oppressor or an authoritative figure is an unusual act in the diegesis; topped with an expressive style that defies narrative conventions of former realist *taşra* films lacking women, and centralising this resistance in its narration, *Mustang* is uncategorisable and excessive. Female resistance for freedom and individuality in the film is interpreted in Turkey as the sisters' depiction of female youth being unrealistic in the story. In fact, *Mustang*'s girls are unique as figures of a girlhood with agency whose desires are not determined by patriarchy; perhaps this kind of girlhood is almost always coded as a threat in political and social discourses, which is reflected in the language of Turkish critiques. Strikingly different from former narrational cinematic strategies in Turkey that are male-centred, such a style is condemned as incompetent and marked as a misconduct of conventional art-house filmmaking in Turkey.

Meanwhile, global reception interprets *Mustang*'s unique style of depicting girlhood as having a global feminist tone or punctuating the universal existence of female agency and sexuality (Abraham 2015; Barnett 2015; Heymann 2015; Fornerod 2015; Nelson 2015; Olszewski 2015; Regnier 2015; Clarke 2016; Tenaglia 2016), and exemplifying exceptional skills in filmmaking (Vié 2015; Weissberg 2015; Crump 2016; Mowe 2016). What the local critics see as an exploitation of female bodies – sometimes to the point of eroticisation, as quoted above – and an exaggeration of patriarchal oppression, is translated as a 'tribute to youth and femininity' and 'an ode to female freedom' (Vié 2015): *Mustang* presents 'laughter [as] an act of resistance' (Heymann 2015); 'it's a moving portrait of sisterhood, a celebration of a fierce femininity and a damning indictment of patriarchal systems that seek to destroy and control this spirit' (Walsh 2015). Unlike their counterparts from Turkey, who claim the presence of a male gaze in Ergüven's directing, international critics defend her cinematography as actually 'subverting [that] gaze' (Colburn 2016): 'Ergüven trains her lens on the girls, half-dressed in pyjamas, lounging about or roughhousing; the goal isn't to sexualise, but rather to depict the relationship each is forming with their own bodies' (ibid). In both English and French reviews, there is an obvious celebration of how the film emphasises 'the girls' unbridled energy, a force that refuses to be locked up, controlled or repressed' (Walsh 2015); *Mustang*'s 'tone and rhythm is brisk, headlong and intelligently lively, like the women at the centre' (Phillips 2016).[4]

The Turkish critical reception, however, entirely ignores this focus on willful girlhood.[5]

Style in *Mustang*, then, is equally appealing to all critics for different reasons. However, its novelty and charm – as acknowledged by both global and local critics – is a consequence of adapting and/or adhering to Western modes of and/or tastes in film aesthetics. Not surprisingly, being 'Western' has different connotations for different writers; yet, in each case, the discussion around Westernness transcends the analysis of the filmic world and the mannerism with which it is constructed. It often involves Ergüven's assumed identity and character traits. 'Visuals are maturely fluent in keeping with current arthouse aesthetics, with a particularly satisfying interplay of energetic and confined camera movements', one reviewer notes, and proposes that 'Ergüven seems to have her eye on the Western market, offering a form of deliverance most Turks with arthouse tastes will find naive at best' (Weissberg 2015). According to another positive review, 'polished and suave Western imagery [is what] gives a universal dimension to a subject that is not limited to the borders of Turkey and the memories of the director's youth' (Omaïs 2015).

In contrast, 'fairy-tale aesthetics'[6] (quoted in Saygılı 2016), a term that Ergüven coins to explain the 'universality' of *Mustang*'s style, is contested by a local critic. He argues that universal is an empty concept, just as 'global audience' is a term used to market these films (ibid.). What they mean with global or universal, he claims, is 'Westerners or pseudo-Westerners who have been brought up with Western knowledge' (ibid.). Indeed, what constitutes 'Western' is ambiguous in these reviews. Seemingly, what makes *Mustang* non-Turkish or foreign is its diversion from the well-known formula of *taşra* films, by adopting an unconventional and non-realist style and being unrepresentative of a previous body of work from Turkey. Moreover, a filmmaking style that is arguably reminiscent of internationally recognised female arthouse directors such as Sofia Coppola[7] and Nadine Labaki – a noticeably recurring comparison in the film's global reception – verifies the claims that the film has the capacity to be 'read easily' by the West, often defined by its 'dreamy', 'lyrical' or 'tale-like' aesthetics found also in its counterparts. These are the same qualities that irritate many writers in Turkey due to the potentially offensive interpretations of fairy-tale reality, that is, producing something 'positive' out of actual sufferings. Life in Turkey, as viewed from the critical body of writing, is almost too sacred to be understood and narrativised from a distant perspective. Meanwhile, the global critical reception is focused on how such stories can be generalised and speak on behalf of many other cultures, if told through a universal language. One reviewer, for instance, describes his experience of understanding the film without understanding the dialogue:

> I knew *Mustang* was a great movie when I first saw it at the Cannes Film Festival in May, without the benefit of English subtitles. Although the film, about five adolescent sisters coming-of-age in a small town on the Black Sea, was entirely in Turkish, it was so dynamic, legible and visually rich that I understood every moment.
> (Hornaday 2016)

The analysis of *Mustang*'s reception makes us question the categorical formulas that exist in festival curating and critical writing for films that exemplify and define 'World Cinema'. Moreover, the efforts to scrutinise the film's Western-ness and accordingly own or reject its story, characters, and style lay bare the ideological positions of the critics, nurtured by a limited, nationalistic understanding of filmmaking. The same efforts indeed expose the processes and properties that determine a film's appropriation of certain contexts and categories. *Mustang* poses a challenge to the existing and often overlapping paradigms of World Cinema, national cinema and transnational cinema with its choices of narrative and narration, as well as production, distribution, and exhibition processes. Elsaesser argues that 'world cinema is often driven by an essentially ethnographic outlook' (2005: 509) and proposes that it 'invariably implies the look from outside and thus conjures up the old anthropological dilemma of the participant observer being presented with the mirror of what the "native" thinks the other, the observer wants to see' (510). Berghahn and Sternberg similarly stress how '[a] particular national cinema [...] can only be included in the World Cinema canon by virtue of its transnational circulation and being appropriated by hegemonic cultures' (2010: 39). Globally recognised or award-worthy examples of national cinemas are often supported by Western funding bodies, making them transnational via their international co-production and reception. Through their journey in international co-funding and exhibition, films made outside the West are approved for Western culture.

Furthermore, Ergüven's gender and migrant identity as well as the film's subject matter of girlhood direct these processes. As Patricia White argues extensively in her book, through examples of world and transnational cinema, 'gender informs not only the images and stories on screen but also the terms of film financing, production, distribution, exhibition and evaluation' (2015: 199–200).[8] *Mustang*'s transnational circulation, for instance, involves discourses of women's rights, conservative politics in Turkey, and aesthetics of women's filmmaking, from its initial scriptwriting development phase until its award and festival selection processes. This is not to say that the film loses value through its journey of completion and reception; on the contrary, we need a more thorough examination of these layers of value and mobility. For global critics, *Mustang*'s categorisation into 'festival/arthouse/world cinema' places more value on the film, while for many local critics such a categorisation demonstrates why *Mustang*'s filmic universe (or Ergüven's authorship) is incapable of representing (or seeing) things as they are 'inside'. Both efforts prove ineffective for bringing out the film's richness and uniqueness because they repeat viewpoints based on binary oppositions; concentrating on the universal aspects of the film or skills of its filmmaker obscures the local details and intricacies that the film puts forward with its stylistic and contextual mannerisms.

Nonetheless, the film owes its popularity in global festivals to its Western-ness, which is reciprocated in its critical reception. Perhaps Western-ness is a quality sought in examples of world cinema that affects a film's viewership, which also proves the often-contested intricate affiliations of festival programmers, critical circles, producers, and distributors whose authority in the international film markets determines the aesthetic value of a cultural product as well its accessibility to different geographies. Consequently, Western-ness may be the name of that universal language forced upon or adopted by a filmmaker in an unspoken and intuitive manner to enter the film market and communicate in it. Quoting Elsaesser, Berghahn and Sternberg remind their reader that this may be 'understood as "symptom of neo-colonialism in the cultural sphere"' (2010: 39).

Transnational Affinities, National Frictions

It is useful at this point to recall Marciniak's paradigm of 'palatable foreignness' (2007) to discuss this said appeal or design of *Mustang* for Western audiences. Drawing on her own experiences as an academic, Marciniak explains palatability as the harmless, non-threatening, and even comforting otherness that is embedded in Western imaginary. She exemplifies the ways in which this understanding is exercised and reassured in institutions' hiring processes and teaching practices as well as representations of foreignness in films. She writes about 'validating experiences of other cultures with the purpose of enriching our own multicultural education' (192) and how 'the foreign is revealed to exist for [our] use' (203). In other words, the mystery, the ambiguity, and the threat that the foreign might trigger in the Western consciousness is effaced by a polished, benevolent version of otherness that carries traces of familiarity, desire, and ease. Ergüven is a 'palatable foreigner' being a Turkey-born, Western-educated resident of France, who is marked as 'exterior' from either geographical position. Likewise, *Mustang* offers a 'palatability' with the kinds of narrative and representational strategies applied in the film, which makes it 'beautiful' and 'culturally unspecific', thus 'easy to watch'. Such strategies, indeed, are attached to Ergüven's in-betweenness and the assumptions around her transnational identity, and often read as influences rather than novelties in the reviews. Dozens of writers, as noted previously, have compared *Mustang* to Coppola's *The Virgin Suicides*, claiming that they have more in common than each film's story being about five sisters' troubles and pains of growing up in a conservative family. Consequently, Ergüven and *Mustang* are neither Turkish, nor French, nor Western enough for anybody. The director's identity and her work offer unmarked territories flexible enough to be categorised as (not) belonging to either one. Instead of approaching her work as having a diversity of positions, the critical reception exposes and emphasises mannerisms in her style that serve the critics' institutionalised position.

For global critics, Ergüven's filmmaking is 'sensitive, humanist, deeply immersive' (Hornaday 2016) and attends its heavy subject matter with 'delicacy and lightness' (Hay 2015), 'joyful energy and enthusiasm' (Périllon 2015). For local critics, however, it exemplifies a 'colonised gaze' (Saygılı 2016) or 'mainstream French culture' (Özakın 2015). Although diverse, all these positions support the idea that 'it is not a coincidence that she receives multiple awards in Europe and competes for the Oscars' (Saygılı 2016). Marciniak writes that the 'monolithic vision of Europe is so deeply ingrained in Western cultural imaginary that most progressive feminist thinkers fall into this trap' (2007: 192). Her criticism is directed at the state of transnational feminist studies; she argues that its global scope is restrictive as it totalises and typecasts diverse groups of women into a single unit. In a similar manner, funders, festivals, and critical circles need tick boxes to enrich the category of world cinema and especially non-Western women's cinema. It is a known fact that investors were not convinced of supporting Ergüven's *Kings* (2017), for its subject matter was deemed too distant from her personal experiences; and she had to start her feature film career with a story derived from her background. Patricia White argues that 'within the festival circuit, singularity is too often co-opted by apolitical discourses of auteurism and national representativeness: this is the paradoxical structural position of the female auteur' (2019: 262–3). 'Western cultural imaginary' is institutionalised in the practice of criticism as well. The value that global reception univocally ascribes to Ergüven is endorsed by her craftiness of depicting female youth, energy, and fearlessness in a patriarchal, conservative environment, as well as the film's affinities with other international examples of contemporary women's cinema. Seemingly, *Mustang*'s style and subject fulfil the criteria necessary to make Ergüven a talent of 'world cinema'.

Meanwhile, the institutionalised notion of national cinema in Turkey is manifested in the film's critical reception as an expectation of a realistic representation of provincial village life. One critic from Turkey disapproving of the attacks against the film not being true to Turkey reads this as an ongoing desire to see a 'pure, romanticised, always longed-for and almost magical *taşra* that has defined the last fifteen years of cinema in Turkey' (Aytaç 2016). Aytaç argues that 'the lack of nostalgia and longing for *taşra* [in *Mustang*] is misread as "directed through Western eyes"' (ibid.). Village and small-town are definitive tropes in films from Turkey, spanning decades of production. Films that are interchangeably called 'local', 'Turkish', or 'national' in Turkish reviews have produced certain conventions and expectations about the image of a small-town or a village; what *taşra* is and how it is represented. Writing in 2002, Suner claims that the provincial small-town serves as 'a site of nostalgia for an imaginary past' (62).[9] In 2021, we might argue that the legacy of *taşra* continues in the cinema of Turkey, with nuances of youthfulness in a handful of films that subvert this image, such as *Ana Yurdu* (Tüzen 2015) and *Kelebekler / Butterflies* (Karaçelik 2018). Neither having a nostalgic tone, nor a realistic representation of the setting, *Mustang* seemingly does not look 'Turkish' enough to critics from Turkey.

Exercising criticism within a dysfunctional and restrictive binary opposition of the West versus Turkey, the local critics' 'This is not Turkey/Turkish' claim is automatically translated into 'This is French/Western'. Universality as a value rarely finds a place in criticism from Turkey because authenticity and verisimilitude are two fundamental criteria that drive most of the arguments.[10] Some film reviews read like assessments of filmic representations through subjective opinions, observations, and experiences of real-life examples. They inquire what it 'actually' means to be female youth in Turkey's provinces and envisage the consequences of many roles and attitudes that the girls assume in the film such as laughing in public, using vulgar language, speaking in a loud voice, and being comfortable with their own bodies. One reviewer accuses the film of depicting contemporary times inaccurately:

The story gives the impression that it takes place in a laboratory environment completely detached from history [...] Frankly, a fiction that depicts today through how our grandmothers got married does not seem convincing; even in the most conservative families couples do not marry each other without at least meeting their family members in a coffee shop.

(Aydemir 2015)

He argues that the film mismatches today's events with the past's as well as being ignorant of local intricacies such as the over-repressive attitudes of the uncle and the grandmother even though they are not portrayed as religious. Some details make the filmic universe far-fetched; 'are we really expected to believe that being a "woman of decency" is accomplished by dressing up as a governess?' he asks (ibid.).

Mustang is satiated with episodes of abuse, oppression, and inequality that do not necessarily support a linear, forward-moving, character-centred narrative. For some critics, this could be criticised as uneconomic and untidy scripting; but instead of explaining this as a matter of technical ineffectiveness, reviewers link it to the film's misreading of Turkey. One reviewer considers the film's 'efforts to marry off three high school girls one after the other, [...] weddings and suicides, sexual harassment, and rambunctious sex in the car in the town square' as 'impositions' in the 90-minute script shaped by an 'effort to say everything possible about one issue to the extent that it damages the sense of reality of the work' (Ercivan 2015). According to another writer, 'the excitement [*Mustang*] created in the international audience and critics is hard to catch in the audience in Turkey. The reason for this is that it over-globalises the difficulties of being a woman in Turkey, which is an issue that should be taken seriously. In doing so, it loses the local audience' (Kural 2015). She continues to argue that 'it is disturbing that the nightmares experienced in the dreamy atmosphere of the film occur within the easy-to-watch tempo of the work: since we know that these nightmares threaten and even end women's lives in Turkey, it feels heavy that the film is visually too "beautiful"' (ibid.). The argument here, then, is that such a delicate and 'true' subject matter should be handled without aestheticising the image. 'Produced according to the global film festival formulas, these films [i.e. films such as *Mustang*] can mesmerise viewers and critics from abroad, but we are aware of the deceptiveness of these projections that claim that they represent us', one critic claims (Şen 2015), and he succinctly reduces the film's interpretive possibilities by writing that 'everything *Mustang* shows about the Turkish type of conservatism and incest, which the film strongly criticises, is materially and morally wrong' (ibid.).

Such reviews, nonetheless, obliviously, or indirectly, contribute to discrimination against women because the language, tone, and argumentations prove that emancipated, sexualised, and willful femininity, even as part of fiction or as a thought, cannot be permitted or tolerated. In these reviews, an inherent hegemonic, patriarchal viewpoint passes as an excuse that *Mustang*'s narrative is unrealistic, its style is aestheticised, or its scripting is not serious. Instead of testing how accurate these filmic representations are with regard to the reality of female youth in provincial villages or small towns in Turkey, one possibility is to attend to the ways in which the film's narrative offers fictionalised spaces exclusively for female subjectivity, as well as engagements with gendered discourses of contemporary politics in Turkey, which Chapters 1 and 2 addressed respectively.

The argument about the film's Western tendency lends itself to unearthing the universal nuances in *Mustang*'s global criticism. The film's handling of its subject matter, some propose, allows it to become a tale of oppression and inequality that many women from around the world experience (Heymann 2015; Nelson 2015; Schumann 2016). '*Mustang* is simultaneously an intimate story of young girls in their home and an extremely all-inclusive tale of female strife in Turkey', one reviewer writes, proposing that 'it serves as a representation of negative treatment of women in any culture [...], a brilliant indictment of tradition itself' (Tenaglia 2016). Others argue that the film depicts 'a courageous fight for the emancipation of women, [...] against intolerance' (Fornerod 2015), 'it could be a cautionary fable about the predatory hypocrisy of any patriarchy, of any community predominantly defined by social conservatism' (Atkinson 2016), and 'it opened a "window of opportunity" for all the women in the world that are gagged, muzzled, even killed every day' (Lajon 2015). Again, these universalist accounts of the film not only resonate with Marciniak's 'palatable foreignness', but also make us recall 'politics of location'. Locating *Mustang* here or there produces misrecognitions and proves ineffective for addressing its multiplicities. It reduces the film to the conventions and expectations of critical discourses founded and preserved within limited ethnocentric geographical and ideological positions. It overlooks the possible readings that could come out of a diverse understanding of the film's transnational production processes, its art-house presence in festivals, its affiliation with national content and context, and the treatment of female agency and coming-of-age within contemporary women's cinema as well as female narratives of female authorship in Turkey.

The critical argument that Marciniak makes about how transnational feminist studies typecasts diversity can be applied to the body of written criticism on *Mustang*, which seemingly homogenises women's issues as global and unitary, and obscures the specific viewpoints that the film offers in relation to female coming-of-age in Turkey. What remains as a valid question to ask through the case of *Mustang*'s critical reception is how 'the geopolitical imaginary of the discipline of film studies [should] be upgraded to a transnational perspective, broadly conceived as above the level of the national but below the level of the global' (Ďurovičová quoted in White 2015: 14). This exercise in un-locating *Mustang* can perhaps open new ways of thinking about films. Co-funding has become a standard practice for a film to join international festival circuits; even entirely nationally produced films that cross their borders and travel the world through film distribution markets and festivals become transnational.[11] Recognising these works within their national context, specific and general festival domains, trends, and tastes, and a broad transnational viewership and reception can perhaps contribute to studies of films as cultural products as well as works of art. Stam's inquiry into 'how cross-border "looking relations" [...] inform the transnational' is helpful for practising such an assessment. He lists a series of questions that could be useful for addressing the differences and overlaps in transnational reception:

> What knowledge can be gleaned from the reciprocal interweavings of the national, the regional, and the transnational by studying what 'passes' from one culture to the other? Why are some genres easily appreciated and understood in some countries but not in others? Are some genres more 'universal' in their appeal, or is their 'universality' premised on the historical 'accident' of Western hegemony and the prior dissemination of western modes and storytelling? Are some themes, such as maternal love for children [...] to be found in [diverse] directors [...] and some genres – e.g. melodrama – intrinsically more transnational in their appeal? [...] Are all genres [...] potentially 'universalizable' once they are supported and disseminated by powerful media institutions and circulation networks?
>
> (2019: 147)

Here, we are cautious about locating *Mustang* anywhere with regard to production, aesthetics, narrative content, or viewership but rather utilise a transnational thinking to reveal the film's potentials. As discussed in previous chapters, *Mustang* is the sole example to date within the cinema of Turkey that pictures a willful girlhood on screen, problematising the female body and sexuality in relation to the contemporary political context and rejecting the realist style of former, male-directed and male-centred, internationally acclaimed films on *taşra*. Hence, the characters, the narrative, and the film's use of a 'light' tone to deliver grave matters are found unconventional, unfitting, or implausible. Neither the film's first-person narration by the youngest sister, suggesting that the viewer see the story from a child's viewpoint, nor its engagement with contemporary politics in Turkey, got much critical attention, both of which are valuable aspects that we attempt to highlight in this book.

Meanwhile, *Mustang*'s transnational aesthetics, its 'universal' subject matter, and festival participations have made it effective to be discussed within the category of transnational feminist world cinema. Seeing 'the national and the transnational as "mutually parasitic" concepts' (Choi quoted in Stam 2019: 140), and, therefore, 'avoid[ing] new binarisms in order to see both national and transnational as mutually invaginated, while also seeing localisation and globalisation as simultaneous and mutually constitutive processes', are helpful in discussing examples like *Mustang*. In this sense, the film has the potential to be interpreted as more than a 'Euro-pudding'[12] (Berghahn and Sternberg 2010: 22) or a 'cinematic McNugget' (Ezra and Rowden quoted in Marciniak, Imre, and O'Healy 2007: 3). Questioning whether to include *Babel* (Iñárritu 2006) as a case among the marginalised, non-canonical transnational examples in their book, Marciniak, Imre, and O'Healy rightly ask:

> Should we [...] oppose *Babel* on principle for rendering the global and the transnational 'trendy'? Should we dismiss its glossy, hyper-real aesthetic surfaces, its violent spectacle, its star appeal, and its success among limousine liberals? Should we deplore it for its Western-friendly sensibility and deem it a 'cinematic McNugget', which deprives the transnational of its critical potential and surrenders it to global capital?
>
> (2007: 3)

Similar to *Babel*, *Mustang* speaks to a diversity of audiences and can be deemed a film that serves the interests of a Western film market with its glossy aesthetics, universal subject matter and light approach to 'reality'. It can be argued that it 'mainstream[s] foreignness and transnationality'[13] (3) and translates many problems that women in Turkey face into bite-sized matters that the viewers can digest and experience with ease. In this sense, *Mustang*'s scripting and production can be contradictory for some – turning the image of oppression into an enjoyable, consumable product – but that does not diminish its critical value. The film problematises women's issues in contemporary Turkey as shared by many scholars, activists, and filmmakers and its potential as a unique example of willful girlhood advocating female sexualities, subjectivities, and agencies should not be dismissed. Affixing such a film's reception to certain institutions of criticism as defined by geographical locations blocks possibilities of interpretation arising from a mix of nation-, culture-, and author-specific qualities. Oscillating between and trespassing national and cultural categories, *Mustang* has the capacity to be read in multiple ways and this quality of in-betweenness makes it a unique example of transnational filmmaking.

Branding Authorship

Transnationalism in *Mustang*, as noted previously, is certainly not detached from Ergüven's authorial persona. Discussing 'the commerce of auteurism', Corrigan writes about 'the marketing transformation of the international art cinema' and argues that 'a director's promoted biography can pre-empt most textual receptions of a movie' (1991: 105). His account of auteurism places emphasis on the commercial value of publicity and promotion. He continues: 'Placed before, after, and outside a film text and its reception, today's auteurs are agents who, whether they wish or not, are always on the verge of being self-consumed by their status as stars' (106). Following his lead, we would like to attempt to evaluate Ergüven's authorial persona depicted in commentaries and critical reviews as a further example of 'mainstreaming of foreignness and transnationality' (Marciniak, Imre, and O'Healy 2007: 3). Looking at interviews and biographical data used in reviews, similar to Corrigan's method of reading three male auteurs, Coppola, Kluge, and Ruiz, we would like to pose questions related to how the (self-)construction of authorial persona contributes to the filmic reception. Moreover, we argue that Ergüven being a woman adds a gendered layer to the critical readings of her filmmaking. Transnational female authorship is a central extra-diegetic component of filmmaking that shapes the interpretation of how the director has handled her subject matter in the film.

In the case of *Mustang*, not only co-production budgets become an issue of nationalist and political discourses, but Ergüven's cultural and social networks and background have been used by critics to assume that her identity shapes her directorial/authorial perspective towards Turkey in the film. Born in Turkey, travelled to various places in the world due to her father's work, settled in France as a teenager, and educated in the renowned film school La Fémis, Ergüven's specific biographical data is used as definitive markers to scrutinise the inclinations in her filmmaking. Indeed, such an approach leads to an individualisation of the filmmaker and the placement of the film into presupposed conventions and expectations. We do not intend to totally dismiss the possible economic, political, and cultural influences of being raised and educated and having produced the film in a diversity of contexts and circles on the style and narrative of this transnational film. We do, however, propose an alternative way of looking at *Mustang* that explores the potentials in Ergüven's filmmaking, which render the repeated binaries of East/West, Turkish/French, female/male and modern/conservative futile in the film's critical evaluation.

Ergüven's 'Franco-Turkishness' is problematised – either deliberately or not, but in a noticeable pattern – to introduce, explain, and prove the film's success and/or popularity, especially in scholarship that came out in France and Turkey. The selection of quotes provided below are exemplary in illustrating the tone and emphasis of these reviews with regard to Ergüven's multiple identities:

> 'I am Turkish'. A remarkable claim for this pretty woman yet very 'global'. Deniz was born in Ankara. Her expression carries the distinction of good schools and the charm of those who speak several languages, thus concealing a mysterious and distant accent [...] 'My dog is French, my husband and my baby'. She also speaks French like you and me, hence the confusion of designating her as Franco-Turkish. In reality, French, she would have liked to become.
>
> (Lajon 2015)

> I wish with all my heart that the film gets the Oscar too. Because even though we don't own it, this film is a Turkish film. All actors are Turkish. The film was shot in Turkey, in İnebolu. It's in Turkish. The director is Turkish [and she] is also the screenwriter. Yes, she has been living in France for many years, but Deniz Gamze Ergüven is Turkish.
>
> (Arman 2015)

> Fluent in Turkish, French and English, she's at home in multiple worlds [...] 'I'm very French and very Turkish', she said. 'I appropriate a lot of different cultures'.
>
> (Donadio 2015)

As evident in the last example, Ergüven emphasises how she oscillates between many cultures and nations, stressing only that she approves of the film culture in France, which she believes embraces diversity (Arman

2015; Kilkenny 2017). She reveals in many interviews the stress and frustration she faced after the Oscar nominations were announced, with regard to the growing discussions around which nation *Mustang* and she herself belonged to (Genç 2015; Richford 2015). Nonetheless, the same interviews in which she describes this concern pose essential questions related to national and cultural belonging. Moreover, the framing of her work, especially by writers outside Turkey, constitutes a layout of elements that make her French. Ergüven's interviews and the film's critical reviews are shaped by marked efforts to prove the Frenchness of Ergüven's success by highlighting her training in La Fémis, *Mustang*'s French co-writer Alice Winocour, and the film's famous producer Charles Gillibert.[14] This information also seems to indicate that the film is worthy of attention as Gillibert is the producer of Cannes-awarded Olivier Assayas, and La Fémis's famous alumni include Celine Sciamma and Claire Denis. Why would a director's education be of significance in a film's critical interpretation? In some texts, her French collaborators and her educational background are mentioned prior to other biographical or production-related information. This is not a typical introduction for a transnational filmmaker. For instance, the biographical background was not a pivotal subject in the reviews of debut feature films directed by transnational directors with Turkish heritage such as Fatih Akın and Ferzan Özpetek.[15] Deniz Gamze Ergüven's status as participant in Cannes and nominee for Oscars with her first feature sparks a gendered reading of her film and a gendered positioning of her directorial style in the global filmmaking sphere.

This positioning is evident in the questions addressed to Ergüven in the interviews as well, which revolve around her identity as a woman. In the narratives of the making of *Mustang*, Ergüven's pregnancy becomes a symbol of discrimination against women on the set; news of her pregnancy seemingly caused the film's former producer to back out of the project.[16] Especially in her *The New York Times* interview, the patriarchal language stands out remarkably:

> After getting a master's degree in African history in Johannesburg, she entered La Fémis in Paris, France's premier film school, where the French director Olivier Assayas led the jury that chose her for its selective directing program. 'Deniz really stood out', Mr. Assayas said. He said her years of trying to get a bigger project off the ground didn't weigh down 'Mustang'. 'It doesn't feel like someone making her first feature', he said. 'It's very confident'.
>
> But 'Mustang' almost fell through. Just weeks before filming was scheduled to begin, a crucial producer pulled out – citing, among

other things, the fact that the director was pregnant and might have trouble keeping to a tight schedule. Alone in a hotel in Istanbul, her cast unaware of the crisis, Ms. Ergüven made frantic phone calls, including to Mr. Assayas. He connected her with his producer, Charles Gillibert, who read the script and immediately signed on.

(Donadio 2015)

Donadio's commentary above constructs Ergüven's success as dependent on two male figures: Assayas's help from her student years is a crucial factor that has led her to meet Gillibert, as he saves *Mustang* from falling apart at the last minute. Regardless of how such details end up in critical writing, whether as a result of Ergüven's own emphasis or the writer's insistence, they become part of her persona and have an impact on the ways in which *Mustang*'s aesthetic, national, and/or cultural properties are constructed and understood.

'The feminist discourse around women directors, especially those from outside the West, challenges the criteria of value upon which traditional notions of auteurism depend', notes Patricia White (2019: 251). Writing about the Chinese director Xiaolu Guo, she argues that there is a tendency to feature non-Western female directors at 'elite international festivals' that shape the taste of international critical circles, and nationality and gender are two criteria that are considered to avoid underrepresentation. She proposes that on top of the interior meaning that writers seek in films to discuss an auteur's style, 'women directors must grapple with the *exterior* meanings imposed by their gender; they are too often defined by person – by looks, by biography – before personality' (254). Moreover, White compares Guo's films to those made by other women filmmakers, including Deniz Gamze Ergüven, Deepa Mehta, and Shirin Neshat, highlighting a common style that mixes accents of exile with unique personal authorial signature (264). White argues that 'such films are often disparaged as "inauthentic" within national contexts, criticised for their efforts to mimic already successful formulas' (258) and that they are reproached for being made to be attractive for foreign tastes, hence external funding. Quoting Amireh and Majaj, Patricia White asserts that 'instead of being received and read as literature, and assessed on literary grounds, Third World women's literary texts have been viewed primarily as sociological treatises granting Western readers a glimpse into the "oppression" of Third World women' (2015: 80).

These observations are acutely valid for Ergüven and evident in *Mustang*'s critical reception. While critics in Turkey reject the representations of rural girlhood as inaccurate, global critics include brief reviews of modernity and women's conditions in contemporary

Turkey, almost as guidelines for reading the film. Consequently, both the film and its filmmaker are trying to surpass the preconceived ideas of nations and cultures. Ergüven's question 'Is it absolutely necessary for films to have a nationality?' (Gürcü 2015a) is applicable to *Mustang*, especially if we are to evaluate this film without bias. Remembering Marciniak's 'palatable foreignness' is useful here, especially her description of the foreign(er)'s use:

> Predictably, the foreign is not imagined as part of the self but as *exteriority* of the self, as the outside, but, even more crucially for my discussion, as 'the not-me but *for-me*' paradigm. That is, the foreign is revealed to exist *for my use* – whether the foreign is understood as a healer of my boredom, a moral example, or a body that cleans up 'my' dirt and is also available for erotic adventures.
> (Marciniak 2007: 203, emphases in original)

The construction of the filmmaker and the interpretation of the film become products of distinct exotic imaginaries, both by local and global critics. The tone and content of the language of the reviews and interviews in Turkish, French, and English, published for a variety of audiences, resonate with the cultural, artistic, and political contexts of their respective locations of publication. Each body of critical writing uses a contextual perspective for either reaffirming or defaming the distinctions of Western education, Western viewpoint, Western aesthetics, and Western lifestyle against their non-Western, Turkish versions. We must be cautious again to recall that the choices of words such as West and Western are necessary to realise the tensions and differences – as quoted in Kaplan above (1994: 138) – between global and local reception, and they are extracted from the body of criticism itself. Turkey, France, and the West are functional discursive terms, and each is a 'unit of analysis *in theory*' (Stam 2019: 40), rather than representing distinct nation-states or nationalities in practice. Nonetheless, the method of reading critical reception in Turkish, French and English reveals shared viewpoints in the assumed positions of writers and viewers from certain geographies as defined within a larger scheme of geopolitics.

Concluding Remarks

While an analysis of *Mustang*'s global reception reveals that it is generally seen as a well-written, well-directed, and highly stylised film that exposes the repression of women globally through a simple story taking place in a village in Turkey, our examination of Turkish critics shows that most of the reviewers rate the film as average and base their criteria of judgement on the film's ability to represent reality. Indeed, (un)-familiarity with the contemporary national context establishes the basis for this separation. Rather than paying attention to the details of the fictional universe and its coherence, local critics evaluate the film through its references to real-life occurrences and experiences, and through its loyalty to locations and characters as known in reality. Therefore, the credibility of the story appears to be a major criterion fabricated by stereotypes, preconceptions, and expectations.

Mustang's global reception, on the other hand, is built on criticism that attends to Ergüven's ability in handling the film's subject matter, the appeal of which lies in its familiar feminist tones coming from characters from a remote setting. According to international critics, this is a film full of female energy protesting against the bigotry, pressure, and abuse of patriarchy and conservatism, while for local critics, the authenticity and credibility of the story is questionable, especially when handled with such vibrant visual style. Seemingly, it is the film's stylistic choices that make it a significant example of world cinema and a promising debut feature from the director, while the same style is found inappropriate, or unrealistic, by local critics for the heavy content that the film explores. While global criticism is shaped by interest and curiosity, local criticism asserts a claim for ownership of the subjects that make up the film's story. In either case, scrutinising the figure of the teenage girl in Turkey is at the centre of these interpretations as an enunciation of ideological discourses such as nationalism, orientalism, and patriarchy, shaped by the geopolitical practices of distribution, exhibition, and viewing.

In critical writings, *Mustang* is understood as 'Ergüven's *Mustang*', not detached from its filmmaker, and the attempts to include it within a single cultural location prove either futile or inadequate. Perhaps this is precisely because of the richness of the film as an example that challenges the definitions of transnational cinema. In surveying the status of women's cinema, Patricia White proposes a methodology that not only looks at authorship, aesthetics, and address, but also production, distribution, exhibition, and reception (2015: 13). In this book, we have followed a similar path. Such an approach allows us to discuss the image of the female youth in Turkey as constructed in the film's universe, its dialogue with the contemporary cultural context and dominant political discourses in Turkey, and the gaps and differences in interpretive practices that may be driven by notions of gender and nationalism as well as power and knowledge relations between cultures. White recalls the first part of a well-known quote (2015: 9) from Claire Johnston's 'Women's Cinema as Counter-Cinema' (1973), which reads: 'In rejecting a sociological analysis of woman in the cinema we reject any view in terms of realism, for this would involve an acceptance of the apparent natural denotation of the sign and would involve a denial of the reality of the myth in operation' (Johnston 1999: 33). Even though Johnston's subject matter was classical Hollywood cinema, the reality of the myth in operation can be translated into the Western imaginary at work in the conceptions of world cinema. Any view in terms of realism is bound to reproduce the constructed myth, in this case, the figure of the teenage girl in Turkey. *Mustang* is neither a film that offers a ground to discuss 'the issue of the difference of the Muslim girl within contemporary France' (Handyside 2019: 367), nor can it be readily dismissed as inauthentic or non-truthful due to the so-called 'auto-ethnographic look' that Ergüven is supposed to bear with her hybrid identity (Cerrahoğlu 2019: 532–3). The discussion in the former case is exemplary of hegemonic Western feminism, which envisages a monolithic, homogeneous Muslim culture bereft of differences and perceives Muslim patriarchal culture as more oppressive – and thus Muslim women as more oppressed and in need of salvation – compared to Western patriarchal models. Even though there are no references to Islam, the Muslim attribute is attached to the figure of the girl, to discuss the right to unveil in France; hence the film's nationality is also attached to it by default. The discussion in the latter case is exemplary of a nationalist stance: it assumes *Mustang*'s style's diversion from a dominant mode of realism leads to a misreading of Turkish culture and society, which is associated with the hybrid cultural background of the filmmaker as a migrant in Europe who does not live in Turkey.

These approaches reduce the film to a limited microcosm of signs and restrict the signified meanings to repetitive discursive positions in reality. Perhaps we can study this film within the framework of what Asuman Suner conceptualises as the 'transnational imaginary' (2007: 66), using *Blackboards* (Makhmalbaf 2000) and *Bulutları Beklerken* (Ustaoğlu 2003) as examples that present a female figure who contradicts the idea of the Middle Eastern woman as understood by Western feminism. She also argues that the 'directors of these films themselves do not perceive their filmmaking practice as limited to the national boundaries of their countries of origin' (ibid.). *Mustang* is hybrid in terms of production: the film cannot be marked within a single nationality. It is this very hybridity that offers an uneasiness, an anxiety about how to approach and interpret the film critically, which reveals the geopolitical, ideological positions of critical institutions. Moreover, the film's diegesis refuses to 'be accurate', just as its narrative is 'too heavy', and the script presents 'too many events' happening to the girls. Because of this loaded script, the film has 'flat characters' whose story is told in a tale-like manner. *Mustang* even carries traces of the 'teen girl film', permeating the aesthetics of 'art-house cinema'. All these features are deemed as flaws in local criticism, making *Mustang* unfitting in the well-established aesthetic register of realist filmmaking in Turkey, dominated by male filmmakers. In contrast, these are some of the points that the film is celebrated for in global criticism, and listed amongst examples of feminist world cinema.

It is our contention that both the local critics' preoccupation with authenticity and verisimilitude, and the global reviews' simplistic celebration of the film as a feminist work flatten *Mustang*'s formal, narrative, and political contribution by reducing it to its national and geographic references. None of these critical approaches individually provides a useful framework for reading *Mustang*. The film's critical reception is a transnationally informed process; and it is 'inherently gendered, sexualised, and racialised' (Marciniak et al., quoted in Stam 2019: 151). The analysis of local and global reception that this chapter offers is a recognition of this categorical criticism and how such approaches fail to contain the diversity and hybridity offered by the film's style and narrative, reducing it to binarisms. It also reveals a serious problem of writing women into film history – would the same conditions apply if *Mustang*'s director were male?

Notes

1 It should also be noted that the film's audiences in Turkey and elsewhere are critically different in size and diversity. *Mustang* was watched by a total of 25,419 people in theatres in Turkey compared to 523,628 in France, reaching up to 1,279,898 in Europe according to the figures from European Audiovisual Observatory (https://lumiere.obs.coe.int/web/film_info/?id=61492; accessed on 26.07.2021). It was placed seventh in its opening week in France, with 81,059 sold tickets, surpassing a Palme d'Or nominee of that year, *Valley of Love* (Nicloux 2015). Considering that Ceylan's Palme d'Or winner *Winter Sleep* (2014) had 344,206 admissions in the previous year, this is a very successful figure for an art film theatrical release in France (https://lumiere.obs.coe.int/web/film_info/?id=47232; accessed on 26.07.2021). Meanwhile, *Mustang* did not become a popular film in Turkey, reaching only a limited festival audience. It had just 8,810 admissions during its opening week as opposed to mainstream films that reached more than 150,000 (https://boxofficeturkiye.com/hafta/detay/2015-43; accessed on 26.07.2021).
2 For data on gender inequality, partner violence, and child marriages, see UN Women's website (https://evaw-global-database.unwomen.org/fr/countries/asia/turkey; accessed on 05.08.2021)

90 *Critical Reception*

3 A cleric, İlhan Şenocak, called the women's national volleyball team members to modesty after their success in the 2020 Olympics (www.al-monitor.com/originals/2021/07/controversial-clerics-modesty-call-turkish-volleyball-team-bounces-back-him; accessed on 29.07.2021).
4 Emphases on 'energy' to describe the youthfulness in the film is highly noticeable in French reception as it recurs in many reviews (Audebert 2015; Barnett 2015; Blottiere 2015; Hay 2015; Heymann 2015; Lizé 2015; Périllon 2015; Regnier 2015; Vié 2015; Pélisson 2017).
5 Few essays are divergent from mainstream writing. Açar's (2015) essay needs mentioning as he founds his criticism on the uncontainable energy of the girls and argues that 'the sole aim is to convert the film into a visual scream for freedom'.
6 Interestingly the word fairy-tale is used to describe *Mustang*'s structure and style in many global reviews; some punctuate this quality by using the word in the titles ('How is *Mustang* Influenced …', Claudio 2016; Kilkenny 2017). Some accredit the 'universalness' of the film to its language and form adopted from tales.
7 It is interesting to note that while dozens of reviews in French and English (Gester 2015; Hoffman 2015; Lemire 2015; Lizé 2015; Vely 2015; Donadio 2016; Maher 2016; Hornaday 2016; Ward 2016 among many others) make reference to *The Virgin Suicides* (Sofia Coppola 1999), only a few in Turkish do (Özgüven 2015; Şen 2015; Alibeygil 2016).
8 Elsaesser (2005), Berghahn and Sternberg (2010), and White (2015) are invaluable resources for thinking about the crossings between world cinema, transnational filmmaking processes, and national cinemas. These studies also expose how ethnicity, race, gender, and nationality inform these categories.
9 Suner proposes that the repetitive trope of 'provincial small-town life' in Turkish cinema 'needs to be analysed within the context of Turkey's integration into the processes of globalisation over the last two decades, an experience of integration that has resulted in anxieties and yearnings built up around the notions of homeland, sense of belonging, and identity' (61). Reviewing three films that came out in 2000 and 2001, she argues that 'the province appears […] as a site of nostalgia for an imaginary past, an idealised representation of the 1970s period accompanied by an indirect critique of the transformation of Turkish society over the last two decades' (62).
10 Dorsay (2015) is one of those rare critics who claims that the film's success is dependent on its universalness, which he links to the difference of 'Europeanness' in *Mustang*, compared to past examples from cinema of Turkey.
11 For a concise and introductory discussion of the complexity of definitions and issues raised around the word 'transnational', see the chapters 'The Transnational Turn', 'Transnational Cinema', 'The Coefficient Transnationality', and 'Transnational Reception, Gender, and Aesthetics' in Stam (2019).

12 According to Berghahn and Sternberg 'Euro-puddings [...] downplay issues of national, ethnic and cultural identity in an attempt to capitalise on (a perhaps synthetic) Europeannes' (2010: 22).
13 Mainstreaming foreignness is something that Marciniak et al. discuss in their introduction in relation to the popular success of *Babel* with its high production value including its internationally acclaimed stars. Politics, problems and perceptions of border crossing are the main subject matter of a film that belongs to the intricate and exclusive networks of transnational neoliberal film production, the nature of which isolates or hinders the possibilities of alternative filmmaking practices that may arise from unique experiences with/against/through borders.
14 'Born in Turkey, trained in France' is the most common introduction for Ergüven, with specific attention to her being a graduate of La Fémis (Audebert 2015; Barnett 2015; Fornerod 2015; Heymann 2015; Lajon 2015; Omaïs 2015; Périllon 2015; Théate 2015; Vely 2015; Vié 2015; Diatkine 2016).
15 Visit the respective IMDb pages to browse the critical reviews listed for *Hamam* (Özpetek 1997) and *Gegen die Wand* (Akın 2004): www.imdb.com/title/tt0119248/externalreviews?ref_=tt_ov_rt and www.imdb.com/title/tt0347048/?ref_=nm_flmg_dr_15.
16 See, for instance, Donadio (2015), Lajon (2015), and Diatkine (2016).

Conclusions

Focusing on director Deniz Gamze Ergüven's debut film *Mustang*, this book adopted diverse modes of critical analysis to explore the film's engagement with style, representation, and spectatorial address in local, national, and transnational frameworks. *Mustang* tells the story of five orphaned sisters living with their grandmother and uncle in a remote Turkish village. Narrating these five characters' rapport with the conservative and segregated gender order through which they are 'trained' for and coerced into arranged marriages, this unconventional coming-of-age story capitalises upon solidarity, willful agency, and resistance rather than a defeatist drama of spectacular victimhood. Yet, since its selection as France's entry for the Best Foreign Language Film at the 88th Academy Awards, the film has received polarised reviews. While the international reviews in the Anglo-American and Francophone circles were celebrating it as a feminist text of rebellion and female empowerment, the Turkish reviews were more sceptical of the film's engagement with the national political context. This book questioned the functions of style, context, and reception by exploring *Mustang*'s ideological operations in terms of national politics, (trans)national feminism, and the theoretical and conceptual frameworks of national/transnational cinemas. We argued that the film's spectacularisation of willful youth and its stylistic evasion of the dominant modes of realism – which shapes the national and international brand of art-house Turkish cinema – result in an interstitial migrant text that does not sit harmoniously with the dominant critical literacies of national film cultures, or with the dominant regimes of palatability in Euro-American circuits of world cinema criticism.

While *Mustang*'s formulation of female agency and subjectivity can be considered as exemplary of new women's narratives in the contemporary cinema of Turkey, the film's stylistic choices reify a transnational feminist accent that does not relate to the local intricacies of gender politics through Turkish cinema's familiar stylistic registers of realism.

DOI: 10.4324/9781003089056-5

We provided an in-depth analysis of *Mustang* to discuss the ways in which style and national reference inform the film's framing of feminist dissent. By critically exploring local and international reviews of the film, we also aimed to address the differences in the criteria with which national and international film critics interpret issues of gender and (trans)nationalism. In addition to its rigorous account of *Mustang*, the book also carried out a critical survey that contextualises images and narratives of youth and girlhood in the cinema of Turkey through their correlations with and responses to the transformative state ideologies.

Mustang's engagement with the female coming-of-age theme can be located within the contemporary global revival of the youth and coming-of-age narratives in contemporary cinema and television. However, this book's framework of 'critical transnationalism' allowed us to adopt a more expansive, multi-scalar approach to *Mustang*'s geographic affiliations. We argued that a critical reading of an interstitial text needs to reflect on its ways of approaching the text's semiotic mobility through its national and transnational features of style, context, and reception. Matching *Mustang*'s international cross-cultural mobility, our account of *Mustang* did not treat national/transnational as a binary opposition but integrated the discursive forces of these categories critically into the film's migratory world.

In the years following *Mustang*'s release, there has been a significant increase of youth-themed narratives in Turkey's cinema. Ranging from popular to alternative cinema, the examples of this recent revival include *Beni Sevenler Listesi / The List of Those Who Love Me* (Erdoğdu 2021), *Sardunya / Geranium* (Bocut 2021), *Bir Nefes Daha / When I am Done Dying* (Dağ 2021), *Yeniden Leyla / Leyla, Once Again* (Hancıoğulları 2020), *İnsanlar İkiye Ayrılır / Two Types of People* (Şahin 2020), *Hayaletler* (Okyay 2020), *Aşk Tesadüfleri Sever 2 / Love Just a Concidence* (Sorak and Sorak 2020), *Biz Böyleyiz / The Way We Are* (Özyurtlu 2020), *Sıfır Bir / Zero Zone* (Taşkın 2020), *Geçen Yaz / Last Summer* (Açıktan 2021), and *Kağıttan Hayatlar / Paper Lives* (Ulkay 2021). To critically reflect on the meanings of this growing cinematic interest in youth, and of their shared discernible narratives and/or stylistic patterns or individualities, a multifaceted approach needs to be implemented. Neither an exclusive focus on national context nor an engagement with global cinematic trends is sufficiently revelatory. Given the recent developments in Turkey that have irreversibly affected the young population (i.e. the severe backlash against gender equality and LGBTQ+ rights on the one hand, devastating economic crisis and class-based struggles on the other), it is noteworthy to explore this proliferation of filmmaking practices revolving around more nuanced and complex portrayals of youth in the national media culture. It is also crucial to delve into potential connections between the distinctive and heterogenous visual and narrative characteristics of these films, and global cinematic trends.

Moreover, it is vital to rethink these examples with regards to the effects of OTT platforms in the media industries. Partly due to Covid-19 preventative measures, and partly due to streaming culture transforming film consumption and viewing habits, a significant number of these examples are screened and/or produced by Netflix, Mubi, or Blutv. Accordingly, the aspects of film narration, genre, style, and form deserve critical attention in parallel with these platforms' own brands and positionings as trendsetters for global youth as a new demographic address. Especially in the case of Netflix, the brand's global criteria and standards very much define both the themes and visual language and style of contemporary youth media.

This changing distribution and production scene also allows media producers to bypass, to a considerable extent, mainstream media regulation and state censorship in Turkey. For instance, documentaries and short films rarely find opportunities to be screened in film theatres outside of film festivals, or on television. Yet young, promising, and award-winning directors' non-fiction features and shorts have been widely shown through these platforms. Also, young directors are commissioned to produce TV series, documentaries, or shorts on these alternative outlets. Productions which do not have a chance to secure mainstream release due to their content and language have a higher chance of being shown on these platforms. However, it is also important to note here that this is a case of 'relative' bypassing of state regulation and censorship. In the case of the Turkish TV series *Love 101*, for example, even Netflix was subjected to censorship, and the gay character of the series was not included in the final script ('Ruling AKP Says …' 2020). Regarding these developments, it becomes clear that any study which approaches youth media today needs to revise and rethink the geographic markers of cultural production (such as national, global, international, and transnational) according to the individualities of the media texts and the intricacies of their contextual belongings and affinities.

Reflecting on Higbee and Lim's critical framework of transnationalism in film studies (2010), Lim discusses 'notable cinematic trends and phenomena that have emerged in the past decade', such as the 'competitive and concessional transnationalism [of Chinese cinema]', 'slow cinema', and 'poor cinema':

Some of these trends are transnational precisely because they are deeply national; or, to put it differently, certain national ambitions can no longer be contained within fixed geographical boundaries as they are increasingly projected onto the global stage and procured through transnational means. Other phenomena do not arise out of any single country but instead have transnational traits that, crucially, do not make recourse to national agendas; they are transnational in spirit – that is, insofar as they either jettison or ignore the national – and they help us rethink the transnational without the national.

(Lim 2019: 1)

Lim's call for a nuanced conceptualisation of transnational filmmaking does not incorporate the changing patterns of contemporary migrant/diasporic filmmaking into its framework. Yet we argue that the established conceptualisations of migrant cinemas in film studies also need readjustments. The post-millennial routes of skilled migration, and the formations of third- and fourth-generation diasporas, result in new forms of cultural expression that do not necessarily reproduce a migrant/diasporic 'accent' (Naficy 2001) invested in familiar narratives of cross-generational conflict, hybridity, modernity-tradition conflicts, racist oppression, or a nostalgia for lost origins. New routes of skilled migration necessitate a revised conceptual framework that effectively accounts for the new interstitial forms of cultural expressions that cannot be 'contained within fixed geographic boundaries' (Lim 2019: 1). Like other examples from binational practitioners featuring various forms of Turkish affiliation on the global stages of film and contemporary arts – such as Kutluğ Ataman's art practice, Ferzan Özpetek's filmmaking (e.g. *La Fate Ignoranti* [2001] and *Sacred Heart* [2005]) and Fatih Akın's later films (e.g. *The Edge of Heaven* [2007], *Soul Kitchen* [2009], and *In the Fade* [2019]) – *Mustang*'s transnationalism and its 'Turkishness' do not allow a critical framework that is built through an exclusively national focus or a narrow diasporic frame. Given the emerging trends of media cultures addressing a demographic construction of 'global youth' as part of 'certain national ambitions [...] [that] are increasingly projected onto the global stage and procured through transnational means' (ibid.), the subject of youth, or of coming-of-age, becomes a powerful narrative tool to articulate new forms of interstitial migrant experiences that liminalise the categorical distinctions between the national and the transnational.

Our approach is informed by other studies that similarly problematise the ineffectiveness of established categories used to address and evaluate transnational films. In their introduction to *Transnational Feminism in Film and Media* (2007), Marciniak, Imre, and O'Healy use the film *Babel* (Iñárritu 2006) as a case study to highlight the complex content, style, and production contexts of similar films as well as the search for terms to define experiences and discourses of 'migrant', 'exilic', or 'diasporic' films and filmmakers. Interpretations attached to these works and their creators assume essentialist views on race, ethnicity, and gender, or similar reflections of a dominant imaginary that immediately marginalises them. The scholars' proposal to think about *Babel* beyond 'the compartmentalising effects that result from the critical dominance of the category of national cinemas' (2007: 9) following Naficy's 'transnational exilic genre' (2001), which 'cuts across previously defined geographic, national, cultural, cinematic, and meta-cinematic boundaries' (Marciniak, Imre, and O'Healy 2007: 9) resonates with our suggestion to move the focus of this discussion to the current complex, widespread and heterogenous migrations of people. Cross-border phenomena have become, and are becoming more multi-directional, fragmented, and textured. Works mentioned above, by Fatih Akın, Ferzan Özpetek, or Kutluğ Ataman, for instance, require a vocabulary that transcends postcolonial, migrant, diasporic or exilic categories, and call for a critical lens that entails a nuanced understanding of migrant authorship by also paying attention to new mobilities such as skilled labour migration, reverse migration, or migration by choice. The complexity in style, content, production, distribution, and exhibition of these films exceeds the parameters of cinema *of* and *in* exile as described by Naficy. This is not to say that these films and filmmakers are completely detached from any national context, but they should be approached individually and without a default branding that conceals their distinctiveness.

Looking at their reception in different countries can demonstrate how problems of intelligibility, verisimilitude, and translation always exist. This certainly applies to *Mustang*, but also to similar films by Shirin Neshat, Marjane Satrapi, Deepa Mehta, and other filmmakers that Patricia White mentions in her study on *Women's Cinema, World Cinema*. Her feminist reading of transnational women's films exposes their inscribed dynamic female collectivity, which, she argues, is obliterated by their categorisation under global art-house cinema:

> I have argued that women's cinema consumed as art cinema compresses into a humanist frame of reception the dimensions of point of view, historical consciousness, political critique, and formal vision that the strong sense of the term 'women's cinema' identifies with feminism, or at least with the female collectivity it

addresses. Despite their positioning for consumption as works about Third World women's oppression in the rhetoric of a problematic global feminism, the best of these films reimagine that collectivity from a transnational perspective. Audiences' desire for culture – aspirational and exotic – is solicited and rerouted by the work and persona of the diasporan woman director.

(2015: 12)

Circulation, funding, and criticism of art-house cinema reduce these films to products for global cinema consumption, while deeper critical engagements may bring out conceptual hinges to position them within a diversity of films, filmmakers, and geographies. A focus on willful female youth throughout the three main chapters in this book has provided such an opportunity.

References

'Abortion is "murder", says Turkey's PM' (2012) *Hürriyet Daily News*, online, 26 May, www.hurriyetdailynews.com/abortion-is-murder-says-turkeys-pm-21665.
Abraham, S. (2015) 'New Film Mustang Explores Young Women's Vitality – and Patriarchy's Brutality', *Bitchmedia*, online, 3 November. www.bitchmedia.org/article/new-film-mustang-explores-young-women's-vitality—and-patriarchy's-brutality.
Acar, F. and Altunok, G. (2013) 'The "Politics of Intimate" at the Intersection of Neo-Liberalism and Neo-Conservatism in Contemporary Turkey', *Women's Studies International Forum*, No. 41, pp. 14–23.
Açar, M. (2015) 'Bir Özgürlük Çığlığı', *Habertürk*, online, 23 October, www.haberturk.com/yazarlar/mehmet-acar/1143761-bir-ozgurluk-cigligi.
Ahmed, S. (2014) *Willful Subjects*, Durham, NC: Duke University Press.
Akbal Süalp, Z.T. (2014) 'Cinema of Thresholds, Without Gravity, Under Urgent Times: Distant Voices, Still Lives', in M. Akser and D. Bayrakdar (eds) *New Cinema, New Media: Reinventing Turkish Cinema*, Newcastle upon Tyne: Cambridge Scholars Publishing, pp. 238–51.
Akbal Süalp, Z.T. (2009) 'Glorified Lumpen "Nothingness" Versus Night Navigations', in D. Bayrakdar (ed.) *Cinema and Politics: Turkish Cinema and the New Europe*, Newcastle upon Tyne: Cambridge Scholars Publishing, pp. 221–31.
Akbal Süalp, Z.T. and Şenova, B. (2008) 'Violence: Muted Women in Scenes of Glorified Lumpen Men', in M. Grzinic and R. Reitsamer (eds) *New Feminism: Worlds of Feminism, Queer and Networking Conditions*, Wien: Löcker, pp. 91–6.
Akçalı, E. (2019a) 'Accented Essays: Documentary as Artistic Practice in Contemporary Audiovisual Works from Turkey', *Critical Arts*, Vol. 33, No. 2, pp. 42–55.
Akçalı, E. (2019b) 'Essayistic Tendencies in Contemporary Kurdish Filmmaking in Turkey', *Journal of Film and Video*, Vol. 71, No. 1, pp. 20–34.
'The AKP's LGBTI history from 2001–2015' (2015) *KaosGL*, online, 28 September, https://kaosgl.org/en/single-news/the-akprsquos-lgbti-history-from-2001-to-2015.

References

Alibeygil, Y.O. (2016) 'İçinden Çıkılamayan İçine Girilemeyen Ev; *Mustang*', *Diren Sanat*, online, 17 January, www.dirensanat.com/2016/01/17/icinden-cikilamayan-icine-girilemeyen-ev/.

Arat, Y. and Pamuk, Ş. (2019) *Turkey Between Democracy and Authoritarianism*, Cambridge: Cambridge University Press.

Arman, A. (2015) 'Yönetmen Türk, hikâye Türk, oyuncular Türk ama Oscar'da Fransa'yı temsil edecek', *Hürriyet*, online, 24 October, www.hurriyet.com.tr/yazarlar/ayse-arman/yonetmen-turk-hik-ye-turk-oyuncular-turk-ama-oscarda-fransayi-temsil-edecek-40005621.

Arslan, S. (2009) 'Venus in Furs, Turks in Purse: Masochism in the New Cinema of Turkey', in D. Bayrakdar (ed.) *Cinema and Politics: Turkish Cinema and the New Europe*, Newcastle upon Tyne: Cambridge Scholars Publishing, pp. 258–67.

Atakav, E. (2014) '"Do One's Dreams Become Smaller As One Becomes Bigger?" Memory, Trauma and the Child in Turkish Cinema', in M. Akser and D. Bayrakdar (eds) *New Cinema, New Media: Reinventing Turkish Cinema*, Newcastle upon Tyne: Cambridge Scholars Publishing, pp. 158–65.

Atkinson, N. (2016) '*Mustang*: A Powerful Film Revealing the Binds of Domestic Prison', *Globe and Mail*, online, 15 January, www.theglobeandmail.com/arts/film/film-reviews/mustang-a-powerful-film-revealing-the-binds-of-domestic-prison/article28193187/.

Atuk, S. (2020) 'Femicide and the Speaking State Woman Killing and Woman (Re)making in Turkey', *Journal of Middle East Women's Studies*, Vol. 16, No. 3, pp. 283–306.

Audebert, P. (2015) '*Mustang*', *Culturapoing*, online, 17 June, www.culturopoing.com/cinema/sorties-salles-cinema/deniz-gamze-erguven-mustang-2014/20150622.

Aydemir, Ş. (2015) '*Mustang*: Masal mı, Deney mi?', *Artful Living*, online, 23 October, www.artfulliving.com.tr/kultur-ve-yasam/mustang-masalmi-deney-mi-i-4084.

Aytaç, D. (2016) '*Mustang*, Bir Zafer', *5Harfliler*, online, 8 January, www.5harfliler.com/mustang-bir-zafer/.

Aytaç, S. and Onaran, G. (2007) 'Search for Identity in City and Province: Istanbul and "the Rest"', *Altyazı – New Prospects on Ambiguous Grounds: Turkish Cinema Now*, November, pp. 18–22.

Barnett, E. (2015) '*Mustang*: une scénographie vitaminée et une incontestable réussite', *Les Inrockuptibles*, online, 12 June, www.lesinrocks.com/cinema/mustang-20816-12-06-2015/.

Beardmore, L. (2016) '*Mustang* is Carrying the Torch for Female Empowerment', *Little White Lies*, online, 11 May, https://lwlies.com/articles/mustang-female-empowerment-turkey/.

Berghahn, D. (2009) 'From Turkish Greengrocer to Drag Queen: Reassessing Patriarchy in Recent Turkish–German Coming-of-age Films', *New Cinemas: Journal of Contemporary Film*, Vol. 7, No. 1, pp. 55–69.

References

Berghahn, D. and Sternberg, C. (2010) 'Locating Migrant and Diasporic Cinema in Contemporary Europe', in D. Berghahn and C. Sternberg (eds) *European Cinema in Motion: Migrant and Diasporic Film in Contemporary Europe*, Basingstoke: Palgrave Macmillan, pp. 12–49.

Blottiere, M. (2015) 'César 2016: *Mustang*, prix du meilleur premier film, un emballant hymne à la liberté', *Telerama*, online, 19 May, www.telerama.fr/festival-de-cannes/2015/mustang-de-deniz-gamze-erguven-un-emballant-hymne-a-la-liberte,126962.php.

Bozkurt, D. (2014) '"Kadın mı kız mı belli değil"in dildeki yeri ve kökeni üzerine', *Birgün*, online, 24 August, https://www.birgun.net/amp/haber/kadin-mi-kiz-mi-belli-degil-in-dildeki-yeri-ve-kokeni-uzerine-67618/.

Bötke, A. (2015) 'Filmekimi 2015 İzlenimleri – Muhafazakârlık Üzerine: *Mustang*', *Fil'm Hafızası*, online, 16 October, https://filmhafizasi.com/filmekimi-2015-izlenimleri-muhafazakarlik-uzerine-mustang/.

Bradbury-Rance, C. (2016) 'Desire, Outcast: Locating Queer Adolescence', in F. Handyside and K. Taylor-Jones (eds) *International Cinema and the Girl: Local Issues, Transnational Contexts*, New York, NY: Palgrave Macmillan, pp. 85–96.

Bradshaw, P. (2017) '*Kings* review – Halle Berry and Daniel Craig Fail to Ignite Baffling LA Riots Drama', *The Guardian*, online, 14 September, www.theguardian.com/film/2017/sep/13/kings-review-halle-berry-toronto-film-festival-tiff.

Braidotti, R. (2008) 'Affirmation, Pain, and Empowerment', *Asian Journal of Women's Studies*, Vol. 14, No. 3, pp. 7–36.

Braidotti, R. (2006) 'Affirmation versus Vulnerability: On Contemporary Ethical Debates', *Canadian Journal of Continental Philosophy*, Vol. 10, No. 1, pp. 235–54.

Buder, E. (2015) 'Meet France's Oscar Entry, "Mustang", a Controversial 5-headed Monster of Femininity', *IndieWire*, online, www.indiewire.com/2015/11/meet-frances-oscar-entry-mustang-a-controversial-5-headed-monster-of-femininity-50271/.

Burul Y. and Eslen-Ziya, H. (2018) 'Understanding "New Turkey" Through Women's Eyes: Gender Politics in Turkish Daytime Talk Shows', *Middle East Critique*, Vol. 27, No. 2, pp. 1–14.

Cerrahoğlu, Z. (2019) 'Sinemada Temsil Kurmak: *Mustang* (2015) Filmi Üzerine Bir İnceleme', *SineFilozofi*, May, Special Issue (No. 1), pp. 518–35.

Ceuterick, M. (2020) *Affirmative Aesthetics and Willful Women: Gender, Space and Mobility in Contemporary Cinema*. Cham: Palgrave Macmillan.

Chareyron R. and Viennot, G. (2019) (eds) *Screening Youth: Contemporary French and Francophone Cinema*, Edinburgh: Edinburgh University Press.

Chion, M. (1999) *The Voice in Cinema*, New York, NY: Columbia University Press.

Cindoglu, D. and Unal, D. (2016) 'Gender and Sexuality in the Authoritarian Discursive Strategies of "New Turkey"', *European Journal of Women's Studies*, Vol. 24, No. 1, pp. 39–54.

References 101

Clarke, C. (2016) 'Mustang', *Time Out*, online, 9 May, www.timeout.com/movies/mustang.

Claudio (2016) 'Mustang – A Dark Turkish Fairy Tale Movie', *I heart Berlin*, online, 24 March, www.iheartberlin.de/2016/03/24/mustang-a-dark-turkish-fairy-tale-movie/.

Colburn, R. (2016) 'Film Review: Mustang', *Consequence*, online, 15 January, https://consequence.net/2016/01/film-review-mustang/.

Colling, S. (2017) *The Aesthetic Pleasures of Girl Teen Film*, New York, NY: Bloomsbury Academic.

Corrigan, T. (1991) *A Cinema Without Walls: Movies and Culture After Vietnam*. New Brunswick: Rutgers University Press.

Coşar, S. and Özkan-Kerestecioğlu, İ. (2017) 'Feminist Politics in Contemporary Turkey: Neo-Liberal Attacks, Feminist Claims to the Public', *Journal of Women, Politics & Policy*, Vol. 38, No. 2, pp. 151–74.

Coşar, S. and Yeğenoğlu, M. (2011) 'New Grounds for Patriarchy in Turkey? Gender Policy in the Age of AKP', *South European Society and Politics*, Vol. 16, No. 4, pp. 555–73.

Crump, A. (2016) 'Mustang', *Paste Magazine*, online, 11 January, www.pastemagazine.com/movies/mustang/.

Çakırlar, C. (2013) 'Aesthetics of Self-Scaling: Parallaxed Transregionalism and Kutluğ Ataman's Art-Practice', *Critical Arts*, Vol. 27, No. 6, pp. 684–706.

Çakırlar, C. (2011) 'Queer Art of Parallaxed Document: The Visual Discourse of Docudrag in Kutluğ Ataman's *Never My Soul!*', *Screen*, Vol. 52, No. 3, pp. 358–75.

Çakırlar, C. and Güçlü, Ö. (2013) 'Gender, Family, and (Home)land in Contemporary Turkish Cinema', in S. Talajooy and K. Laachir (eds) *Resistance in Contemporary Middle Eastern Cultures: Literature, Cinema and Music*, London: Routledge, pp. 167–83.

Çınar, A. (2019) 'Negotiating the Foundations of the Modern State: The Emasculated Citizen and the Call for a Post-Patriarchal State at Gezi Protests', *Theory and Society*, Vol. 48, pp. 453–82.

Çiçekoğlu, F. (2019) *İsyankar Şehir: Gezi Sonrası İstanbul Filmlerinde Mahrem-İsyan*, İstanbul: Metis Yayınları.

Daldal, A. (2015) 'Mustang', *BirGün Pazar*, online, 1 November, www.birgun.net/haber/mustang-93951.

Debruge, P. (2015) '10 Directors to Watch: Deniz Gamze Erguven's "Mustang" is France's Horse in Oscar Race', *Variety*, online, 29 December, https://variety.com/2015/film/features/10-directors-to-watch-deniz-gamze-erguven-mustang-1201668756/.

Diatkine, A. (2016) 'Deniz Gamze Ergüven, au galop', *Libération*, online, 23 February, www.liberation.fr/cinema/2016/02/23/deniz-gamze-erguven-au-galop_1435351/.

Doane, M. A. (1985) 'The Voice in Cinema: The Articulation of Body and Space', in E. Weis and J. Belton (eds) *Film Sound*, New York, NY: Columbia University Press, pp. 162–76.

References

Donadio, R. (2016) 'Son of Saul Leads Foreign Language Race, but Look Out for Mustang', The New York Times, online, 23 February, www.nytimes.com/2016/02/24/movies/son-of-saul-leads-foreign-language-race-but-look-out-for-mustang.html.

Donadio, R. (2015) 'With Mustang, a Director Breaks Free of Cultural Confines', The New York Times, online, 18 November, www.nytimes.com/2015/11/22/movies/with-mustang-a-director-breaks-free-of-cultural-confines.html.

Dorsay, A. (2015) 'Görkemli bir kadın filmi, bir çağdaş sinema başyapıtı', T24, online, 23 October, https://t24.com.tr/yazarlar/atilla-dorsay/gorkemli-bir-kadin-filmi-bir-cagdas-sinema-basyapiti,13009.

Dönmez-Colin, G. (2004) Turkish Cinema: Identity, Distance and Belonging, London: Reaktion Books.

Driscoll, C. (2011) Teen Film: A Critical Introduction, Oxford: Berg.

Driscoll, C. (2002) Girls: Feminine Adolescence in Popular Culture and Theory, New York, NY: Columbia University Press.

Durakbaşa, A. and Karapehlivan, F. (2018) 'Progress and Pitfalls in Women's Education in Turkey (1839–2017)', Encounters in Theory and History of Education, Vol. 19, pp. 70–89.

Düzcan, E. (2017) 'Yeni Türkiye Sinemasında Yetişkinliğe Geçiş: Sivas ve Hayat Var Filmlerinde Cinsiyet, Güç ve Oyun', Akdeniz Üniversitesi İletişim Fakültesi Dergisi, Vol. 28, pp. 142–61.

'Efkan Ala da hedef gösterme peşinde: Eşcinsel evlilik insanlığın helakıdır' (2015) Birgün, online, 2 June, www.birgun.net/haber/efkan-ala-da-hedef-gosterme-pesinde-escinsel-evlilik-insanligin-helakidir-82104.

Elsaesser, T. (2005) European Cinema: Face to Face with Hollywood, Amsterdam: Amsterdam University Press.

Ercivan, A. (2015) 'Mustang', Beyazperde, online, 23 October, www.beyazperde.com/filmler/film-228825/.

'Erdogan Wants to Snoop in Student Bedrooms' (2013) DW Europe, online, 15 November, www.dw.com/en/erdogan-wants-to-snoop-in-student-bedrooms/a-17230991.

Eslen-Ziya, H. and Kazanoğlu, N. (2022) 'De-Democratization under the New Turkey? Challenges for Women's Organisations', Mediterranean Studies, Vol. 27, No. 1, pp. 101–22.

'Evliliği geciktirmeyin, TÜRGEV bu konuda çok iyi bir ihtisas alanı' (2014) T24, online 18 July, https://t24.com.tr/haber/evliligi-geciktirmeyin-turgev-bu-konuda-cok-iyi-bir-ihtisas-alani,264790.

FIAFNY (2016) 'Mustang Q&A with Director and Lead Actresses', YouTube, online, 26 February, www.youtube.com/watch?v=GnnGKqLh9ks.

Fornerod, P. (2015) 'Quand de jeunes Turques roulent en Mustang', Ouest France, online, 17 June, www.ouest-france.fr/culture/cinema/cinema-quand-de-jeunes-turques-route-en-mustang-3488509.

Genç, M. (2015) 'Mustang'in yönetmeni: Türkiye'de birazcık daha sahiplenilmeyi umardım', Radikal, online, 3 November, www.radikal.com.tr/kultur/mustangin-yonetmeni-turkiyede-birazcik-daha-sahiplenilmeyi-umardim-1465544/.

References

Gester, J. (2015) '*Mustang*, les cinq sœurs enfermées de l'intérieur', *Libération*, online, 16 June, www.liberation.fr/cinema/2015/06/16/mustang-les-cinq-soeurs-enfermees-de-l-interieur_1331027/.

Gopinath, G. (2005) *Impossible Desires: Queer Diasporas and South Asian Public Cultures*, Durham, NC: Duke University Press.

Gökçe, Ö. (2009) '(Cannot) Remember: Landscapes of Loss in Contemporary Turkish Cinema', in D. Bayrakdar (ed.) *Cinema and Politics: Turkish Cinema and the New Europe*, Newcastle upon Tyne: Cambridge Scholars Publishing, pp. 268–79.

Güçlü, Ö. (2017) 'Kocan Kadar Konuş ya da Son Dönem Türkiye Sinemasının "Hayırlısıyla" Bekar Kadın Karakter Hizalaması', *Kültür ve İletişim*, Vol. 20, No. 39, pp. 186–209.

Güçlü, Ö. (2016) *Female Silences, Turkey's Crises: Gender, Nation and Past in the New Cinema of Turkey*, Newcastle upon Tyne: Cambridge Scholars Publishing.

Güçlü, Ö. (2011) 'My Only Sunshine / Hayat Var (2008)', in Ö. Köksal (ed.) *World Film Locations: Istanbul*, Bristol: Intellect, pp. 86–7.

Gürbilek, N. (2001) *Kötü Çocuk Türk*, Istanbul: Metis.

Gürcü, D. (2015a) 'Deniz Gamze Ergüven' in Fransa'dan Oscar Aday Adayı olan *Mustang* destanı', *T24*, online, 24 October, https://t24.com.tr/yazarlar/dilara-gurcu/deniz-gamze-erguvenin-fransadan-oscar-aday-adayi-olan-mustang-destani,13026.

Gürcü, D. (2015b) 'In Turkey Girls Aren't Raised to be Heroines', *Dilara Gürcü*, online, 24 October, https://dilaragurcu.wordpress.com/2017/03/04/in-turkey-girls-arent-raised-to-be-heroines/.

Handyside, F. (2019) 'The Politics of Hair: Girls, Secularism and (Not) the Veil in *Mustang* and Other Recent French Films', *Paragraph*, Vol. 42, No. 3, pp. 351–69.

Hay, J-C. (2015) '*Mustang*: un vent de liberté', *Gala*, online, 19 May, www.gala.fr/l_actu/culture/mustang_un_vent_de_liberte_341962.

Henderson, O. (2018) '*Kings*', *RogerEbert.com*, online, 28 April, www.rogerebert.com/reviews/kings-2018.

Heymann, D. (2015) '*Mustang* et ses indomptables', *Marianne*, online, 19 June, www.marianne.net/culture/mustang-et-ses-indomptables.

Higbee, W. and Lim, S. H. (2010) 'Concepts of Transnational Cinema: Towards a Crucial Transnationalism in Film Studies', *Transnational Cinemas*, Vol. 1, No. 1, pp. 7–21.

Hoffman, J. (2015) '*Mustang* review: The Virgin Suicides in Anatolia is a Sweet, Sad Turkish Delight', *The Guardian*, online, 19 May, www.theguardian.com/film/2015/may/19/mustang-review-the-virgin-suicides-in-istanbul-is-a-turkish-delight.

'Homosexuality is a Disease Says Turkish Minister' (2010) *KaosGL*, online, 8 March, https://kaosgl.org/en/single-news/homosexuality-is-a-disease-says-turkish-minister.

Hornaday, A. (2016) '*Mustang* Features Beguiling Stars in a Dynamic and Well-Crafted Story', *Washington Post*, online, 14 January, www.washingtonpost.com/goingoutguide/movies/mustang-features-beguiling-stars-in-a-dynamic-and-well-crafted-story/2016/01/14/721f7d7c-ba14-11e5-829c-26ffb874a18d_story.html.

'How is *Mustang* Influenced by Fairy Tales?' (no date), *The Take*, online, https://the-take.com/watch/how-is-mustang-influenced-by-fairy-tales.

Johnston, C. (1999) 'Women's Cinema as Counter-Cinema', in S. Thornham (ed.) *Feminist Film Theory: A Reader*, Edinburgh: Edinburgh University Press, pp. 31–40 (originally published in 1973).

Kandiyoti, D. (2016) 'Locating the Politics of Gender: Patriarchy, Neo-liberal Governance and Violence in Turkey', *Research and Policy on Turkey*, Vol. 1, No. 2, pp. 103–18.

Kaplan, C. (1994) 'The Politics of Location as Transnational Feminist Critical Practice', in E. Grewal and C. Kaplan (eds) *Scattered Hegemonies: Postmodernity and Transnational Feminist Practices*, Minneapolis, MN: University of Minnesota Press, pp. 137–52.

Kilkenny, K. (2017) '*Mustang*: A Feminist Fairy Tale Sticks it to The Turkish Patriarchy', *Pacific Standard*, online, 14 June, https://psmag.com/social-justice/hope-this-wins-over-son-of-saul/.

Konda (2014) *Gezi Raporu*, online, June, https://konda.com.tr/tr/rapor/gezi-raporu/.

Korkman, Z. (2016) 'Politics of Intimacy: A Distraction of "Real" Politics?', *Journal of Middle East Women's Studies*, Vol. 12, No. 1, pp. 112–21.

Korkman, Z. (2015) 'Blessing Neoliberalism: Economy, Family, and the Occult in Millennial Turkey', *Journal of the Ottoman and Turkish Studies Association*, Vol. 2, No. 2, pp. 335–57.

Korkut, U. and Eslen-Ziya, H. (2016) 'The Evolution of Pro-Birth Regime in Turkey: Discursive Governance of Population Politics', *Social Politics: International Studies in Gender, State and Society*, Vol. 23, No. 4, pp. 555–75.

Kristeva, J. (2014) 'New Forms of Revolt', *Journal of French and Francophone Philosophy*, Vol. 22, No. 2, pp. 1–19.

Kristeva, J. (2002) *Intimate Revolt: The Powers and Limits of Psychoanalysis*, New York, NY: Columbia University Press (originally published in 1997).

Kural, N. (2015) 'Evrensele ulaştı ama yerele hitap edecek mi?', *Milliyet*, online, 24 October, www.milliyet.com.tr/yazarlar/nil-kural/evrensele-ulasti-ama-yerele-hitap-edecek-mi-2136866.

Lajon, K. (2015) 'Deniz Gamze Ergüven, cinéaste, turque et libre', *Le Journal du Dimanche*, online, 30 May, www.lejdd.fr/International/Moyen-Orient/Deniz-Gamze-Ergueven-cineaste-turc-et-libre-735066.

Lemire, C. (2015) '*Mustang*', *RogerEbert.com*, online, 20 November, www.rogerebert.com/reviews/mustang-2015.

Liktor, C. (2021) 'Ufuksuz Bir Dünyada', *Altyazı*, No. 206, online, https://altyazi.net/dergi/sayi/206/206-ufuksuz-bir-dunyada.

Lim, S.H. (2019) 'Concepts of Transnational Cinema Revisited', *Transnational Screens*, Vol. 10, No. 1, pp. 1–12.

Lizé, H. (2015) '*Mustang*: elles ruent dans les brancards', *Le Parisien*, online, 17 June, www.leparisien.fr/culture-loisirs/cinema/mustang-elles-ruent-dans-les-brancards-17-06-2015-4869309.php.

References

Lüküslü, D. (2016) 'Creating a Pious Generation: Youth and Education Policies of the AKP in Turkey', *Southeast European and Black Sea Studies*, Vol. 16, No. 4, pp. 637–49.

Maher, K. (2016) '*Mustang*', *Times*, online, 13 May, www.thetimes.co.uk/article/mustang-jrqzz23sl.

Marciniak, K. (2007) 'Palatable Foreignness', in I. Marciniak, A. Imre and Á. O'Healy (eds) *Transnational Feminism in Film and Media*, New York, NY: Palgrave Macmillan, pp. 187–203.

Marciniak, K., Imre, A. and O'Healy, Á. (2007) 'Introduction', in I. Marciniak, A. Imre and Á. O'Healy (eds) *Transnational Feminism in Film and Media*, New York, NY: Palgrave Macmillan, pp. 1–18.

Martin, A. (1994) *Phantasms: The Dreams and Desires at the Heart of Our Popular Culture*, Melbourne: McPhee Gribble.

Martin, A. (1989) 'The Teen Movie: Why Bother?', *Cinema Papers*, Vol. 75, No. 12, pp. 1–19.

Mowe, R. (2016) '*Mustang*', *Eye for film*, online, 28 January, www.eyeforfilm.co.uk/review/mustang-2015-film-review-by-richard-mowe/.

Naficy, H. (2001) *An Accented Cinema: Exilic and Diasporic Filmmaking*, Princeton, NJ: Princeton University Press.

Naficy, H. (1999) 'Between Rocks and Hard Places: The Interstitial Mode of Production in Exilic Cinema', in H. Naficy (ed.) *Home, Exile, Homeland: Film, Media and the Politics of Place*, London: Routledge, pp. 125–47.

Nelson, J. (2015) '*Mustang*', *DVD Talk*, online, 20 November, www.dvdtalk.com/reviews/70023/mustang-afi-fest-2015/.

Olszewski, T. (2015) '*Mustang* Review: France's Oscar Entry Offers Five Sisters With a Singular Bond', *Wrap*, online, 21 November, www.thewrap.com/mustang-review-france-oscar-turkey-academy-awards/.

Omaïs, M. (2015) '3 bonnes raisons de craquer pour les jeunes héroïnes de *Mustang*', *LCI*, online, 16 June, www.lci.fr/cinema/3-bonnes-raisons-de-craquer-pour-les-jeunes-heroines-de-mustang-1525013.html.

'Over Half of Turks Support Forbidding Co-Ed Student Housing, Poll Shows' (2013), *Hürriyet Daily News*, online, 2 December www.hurriyetdailynews.com/over-half-of-turks-support-forbidding-co-ed-student-housing-poll-shows-58827.

Özakın, Ü. (2015) 'Mustang filmine dair bir feminist okuma denemesi: feminist filme sızan erkek bakışı', *amargi*, online, 3 December, www.amargidergi.com/yeni/?p=1700.

Özgüven, F. (2015) 'FilmEkimi Notları', *fozguven.blogspot.com*, online, 8 October, http://fozguven.blogspot.com/2015/10/filmekimi-notlari-mustang-bir-enerjiyle.html.

Öztan, E. (2014) 'Domesticity of Neoliberalism: Family, Sexuality and Gender in Turkey', in İ. Akça, A. Bekmen and B.A. Özden (eds) *Turkey Reframed: Constituting Neoliberal Hegemony*, London: Pluto Press, pp. 174–87.

Pamak, G. (2019) 'Yeşilçam'dan Arabesk'e Türkiye Sinemasının Çocuk Tahayyülü', *Türk Film Araştırmalarında Yeni Yönelimler*, No. 15, pp. 143–60.

Pélisson, O. (2017) '*Mustang*: une vitalité débordante', *Bande a part*, online, 18 May, www.bande-a-part.fr/cinema/critique/critique-mustand-deniz-gamze-erguven-julieta-diaz-sebastian-molinaro-marta-lubos-magazine-de-cinema/.

Périllon, T. (2015) '*Mustang*', *Le Bleu du Miroir*, online, 17 May, www.lebleudumiroir.fr/mustang/.

Phillips, M. (2016) '*Mustang* review: 5 Teens Search for a Way Out of their Turkish Village', *Chicago Tribune*, online, 14 January, www.chicagotribune.com/entertainment/movies/sc-mustang-movie-review-turkey-0111-20160114-column.html.

Rancière, J. (2010) 'The Paradoxes of Political Art', *Dissensus: On Politics and Aesthetics*, London: Continuum, pp. 134–51.

Regnier, I. (2015) '*Mustang*: cinq filles au galop', *Le Monde*, online, 19 May, www.lemonde.fr/festival-de-cannes/article/2016/04/01/mustang-cinq-filles-au-galop_4636657_766360.html.

Richford, R. (2015) '*Mustang* Director on How France's Turkish-Language Oscar Submission Straddles Two Cultures', *Hollywood Reporter*, online, 14 December, www.hollywoodreporter.com/movies/movie-news/mustang-director-how-frances-turkish-847403/.

'Ruling AKP Says Character in Netflix Series "Love 101" Was Originally Gay, Confessing to Censorship' (2020), *duvaR.english*, online, 7 July, www.duvarenglish.com/domestic/2020/07/07/ruling-akp-confesses-to-govt-censorship-on-love-101-scenario.

Saygılı, K. (2016) '*Mustang* (2015): Sömürgeleştirilmiş Bakış'ın Şaşırtmayan Oscar Yolculuğu', *Cineritüel*, online, 24 February, www.cinerituel.com/mustang-2015-somurgelestirilmis-bakisin-sasirtmayan-oscar-yolculugu/.

Schumann, H. (2016) 'Movie Review: *Mustang* (2015)', *Critical Critics*, online, 4 June, https://thecriticalcritics.com/reviews/movie-review-mustang/.

Sedgwick, E.K. (1990) *Epistemology of the Closet*, Berkeley, CA: University of California Press.

Shary, T. (2014) *Generation Multiples: The Image of Youth in Contemporary American Cinema*, Austin, TX: University of Texas Press.

Shary, T. (2004) *Teen Movies: American Youth on Screen*, New York, NY: Wallflower Press.

Shary, T. and Seibel, A. (2007) (eds) *Youth Culture in Global Cinema*, Austin, TX: University of Texas Press.

Silverman, K. (1988) *The Acoustic Mirror: The Female Voice in Psychoanalysis and Cinema*, Bloomington, IN: Indiana University Press.

Smith, F. (2020) *Bandes de Filles: Girlhood Identities in Contemporary France*, London: Routledge.

Smith, F. (2017) *Rethinking the Hollywood Teen Movie*, Edinburgh: Edinburgh University Press.

Stam, R. (2019) *World Literature, Transnational Cinema, and Global Media*, London: Routledge.

Suner, A. (2010) *New Turkish Cinema: Belonging, Identity and Memory*, New York, NY: I.B. Tauris.

References 107

Suner, A. (2007) 'Cinema without Frontiers: Transnational Women's Filmmaking in Iran and Turkey', in I. Marciniak, A. Imre, and Á. O'Healy (eds) *Transnational Feminism in Film and Media*, New York, NY: Palgrave Macmillan, pp. 53–70.

Suner, A. (2004) 'Horror of a Different Kind: Dissonant Voices of the New Turkish Cinema', *Screen*, Vol. 45, No. 4, pp. 305–23.

Suner, A. (2002) 'Nostalgia for an Imaginary Home: Memory, Space, and Identity in the New Turkish Cinema', *New Perspectives on Turkey*, No, 27, Fall, pp. 61–76.

Şen, M.T. (2015) 'Mustang Üzerinde Ödül Avcılığı Yapmak!', *CİNEDERGİ*, online, 30 November, www.cinedergi.com/2015/11/30/mustang-uzerinde-odul-avciligi-yapmak/.

Tenaglia, R. (2016) '*Movie Review:* Mustang', *CinemaNerdz*, online, 2 February, https://cinemanerdz.com/movie-review-mustang/.

Théate, B. (2015) '*Mustang* nommé dans la course à l'Oscar du meilleur film en langue étrangère', *Le Journal du Dimanche*, online, 14 June, www.lejdd.fr/Culture/Cinema/Les-fougueuses-amazones-turques-de-Mustang-737598.

'Turkey's President Erdoğan Claims To Have Never Interfered With Anyone's Lifestyles' (2017) *Birgün*, online, 5 January, www.birgun.net/haber/turkey-s-president-erdogan-claims-to-have-never-interfered-with-anyone-s-lifestyles-142115.

'Turkish PM Erdoğan Reiterates His Call for Three Children' (2013), *Hürriyet Daily News*, online, 3 January, www.hurriyetdailynews.com/turkish-pm-erdogan-reiterates-his-call-for-three-children-38235.

'Turkish President Says Childless Women Are "Deficient" and "Incomplete"' (2016) *Guardian*, online, 6 June, www.theguardian.com/world/2016/jun/06/turkish-president-erdogan-childless-women-deficient-incomplete.

'Turkish President Erdoğan Says Gender Equality Against Nature' (2014), *Hürriyet Daily News*, online, 4 November, www.hurriyetdailynews.com/turkish-president-erdogan-says-gender-equality-against-nature-74726.

'Turkish President Erdoğan Says There is "No Such Thing as LGBT"' (2021), *Daily Mail*, online, 5 February, www.dailymail.co.uk/news/article-9225327/Turkish-President-Erdogan-says-no-thing-LGBT-amid-protests.html.

'Turkish TV Presenter Fired over Low-Cut Dress after Criticism from AKP Spokesman' (2013), *Hürriyet Daily News*, online, 8 October, www.hurriyetdailynews.com/turkish-tv-presenter-fired-over-low-cut-dress-after-criticism-from-akp-spokesman-55896.

Turner, R. (2006) '"How Do You Know She is a Woman?"', in J. Luchjenbroers (ed.) *Cognitive Linguistics Investigations: Across Languages, Fields and Philosophical Boundaries*, Amsterdam: John Benjamin Publishing Company, pp. 219–34.

Ulusay, N. (2004) 'Günümüz Türk Sinemasında "Erkek Filmleri"nin Yükselişi ve Erkeklik Krizi', *Toplum ve Bilim*, No. 101, pp. 144–61.

Vardan, U. (2015) 'Genel resim doğru ama…', *Hürriyet*, online, 24 October, www.hurriyet.com.tr/yazarlar/ugur-vardan/genel-resim-dogru-ama-40005458.

Vely, Y. (2015) '*Mustang*: la critique', *Paris Match*, online, 16 June, www.parismatch.com/Culture/Cinema/Mustang-la-critique-766054.

Vié, C. (2015) '*Mustang*, un *Virgin Suicides* turc? La réalisatrice du film conteste la comparaison', *20 Minutes*, online, 17 June, www.20minutes.fr/cinema/1628663-20150617-mustang-virgin-suicides-turc-realisatrice-film-conteste-comparaison.

Walsh, K. (2015) '*Mustang* a Moving Portrait of Turkish Sisters' Unbridled Energy and Fierce Femininity', *Chicago Tribune*, online, 19 November, www.chicagotribune.com/la-et-mn-mustang-20151120-story.html.

Ward, S. (2016) 'Sisters Doing it for Themselves: Ergüven's *Mustang*', *Metro*, No. 189, pp. 70–5.

'"We do exist": Turkey's LGBT Community Anxious but Defiant in the Face of Fresh Gov's Attacks' (2021) *duvaR.english*, online, 3 February, www.duvarenglish.com/we-do-exist-turkeys-lgbt-community-anxious-but-defiant-in-the-face-of-fresh-govt-attacks-news-56107.

Weissberg, J. (2015) 'Film Review: *Mustang*', *Variety*, online, 19 May, https://variety.com/2015/film/festivals/mustang-review-cannes-1201500486/.

White, P. (2019) 'She, a Chinese Director? Xiaolu Guo and Transnational Feminist Authorship', in I. Margulies and J. Szaniawski (eds) *On Women's Films: Across Worlds and Generations*, London: Bloomsbury, pp. 251–66.

White, P. (2015) *Women's Cinema, World Cinema: Projecting Contemporary Feminisms*, Durham, NC: Duke University Press.

Wilson, E. (2021) *Céline Sciamma: Portraits*, Edinburgh: Edinburgh University Press.

'Women Should Not Laugh in Public, Turkish Deputy PM Says' (2014) *Hürriyet Daily News*, online, 29 July, www.hurriyetdailynews.com/women-should-not-laugh-in-public-turkish-deputy-pm-says--69732.

Wyatt, J. (2019) *The Virgin Suicides: Reverie, Sorrow and Young Love*, London: Routledge.

Yatçi, D. (2022) 'Toplumun Sopasına Karşı: İnatçı Kızlar ve İcat Ettikleri Yeni Kapılar', *5Harfliler*, online, 18 February, www.5harfliler.com/toplumun-sopasina-karsi-inatci-kizlar-ve-icat-ettikleri-yeni-kapilar/.

Index

Note: Page numbers in *italics* indicate a figure on the corresponding page. Page numbers followed by 'n' indicate a note.

2 Genç Kız / 2 Girls (Ataman 2005) 6, 7, *8*, 43, 46, 59, 63

accented: aesthetics 2; cinema 14–15; style 68
Acıların Çocuğu / The Child of Pains (Efekan 1985) 4
Affirmative Aesthetics and Willful Women: Gender, Space and Mobility in Contemporary Cinema 42
affirmative ethics 17–18
Ahlat Ağacı / The Wild Pear Tree (Ceylan 2018) 9, 46, 59
Ahmed, Sara 5–10, 37, 40, 42, 43, 46, 47, 48, 62; *see also* willful; willfulness
Akın, Fatih 42, 84, 95, 96
AKP (Justice and Development Party) 7, 11, 18, 20, 25–7, 31, 35; gender politics 11, 29, 31, 32; ideals of 'proper' youth 32; sexist public statements 27, 29; *see also* familialism; LGBTQ+; New Turkey; pious generation; speaking state; 'wife-factory'
al-Mansour, Haifa 42
American Honey (Arnold 2016) 11
Ana Yurdu / Motherland (Tüzen 2015) 34, 38, 59, 77
Annemin Şarkısı / My Mother's Song (Mintaş 2014) 6
anti-feminism 11, 18, 25
anti-feminist 22; discourses 19, 27; statements 29

arabesk films 4, 58–9
Arada / In Between (Tunç 2018) 6, 46
Arınç, Bülent 28; statement on women's laughter 31
art-house: cinema 13–14, 89, 92, 96–7; distribution 15, 17; films 11, 15; look 19, 67–8; style 1, production 21, 33
Aşk, Büyü vs. / Love, Spell and All That (Ünal 2019) 34, 35
Aşk Tesadüfleri Sever 2 / Love Just a Coincidence (Sorak and Sorak 2020) 93
Asmalı Konak: Hayat / Ivy Mansion: Life (Oğuz 2003) 33
Assayas, Olivier 84–5
Ataman, Kutluğ 6, 43, 63, 95–6
Atlıkarınca / Merry-Go-Round (Başarır 2010) 34, 35, 38
Atuk, Sumru 29; *see also* speaking state
authorship 13–17; cross-cultural 57; diasporic 2; female 79, 82–6; interstitial 6, 57; migrant 96
Ayrılamam (1986) 5
Ayşecik Canımın İçi / Ayşecik My Dearest (Saner 1963) 3
Ayşecik Cimcime Hanım / Ayşecik Naughty Lady (Saner 1964) 3
Ayşecikle Ömercik (1969) 5
Ayşecik Sokak Kızı / Ayşecik Street Girl (Erakalın 1966) 3

Babamın Sesi / *Voice of My Father* (Eskiköy 2015) 7
Babel (Iñárritu 2006) 81, 91n13, 96
Bal / *Honey* (Kaplanoğlu 2010) 52, 68
Balcı, Emine Emel 6, 43
Başka Semtin Çocukları / *Children of the Otherside* (Bulut 2008) 6, 46, 53
Beni Bende Bitirdiler (Saydam 1989) 4
Beni Sevenler Listesi / *The List of Those Who Love Me* (Erdoğdu 2021) 93
Beş Vakit / *Times and Winds* (Erdem 2006) 52
Bilmemek / *Not Knowing* (Yılmaz 2019) 6
Bir Nefes Daha / *When I am Done Dying* (Dağ 2021) 93
Biz Böyleyiz / *The Way We Are* (Özyurtlu 2020) 93
Blackboards (Makhmalbaf 2000) 88
Blue is the Warmest Colour (Kechiche 2013) 11
Bornova Bornova (Temelkuran 2009) 6
Boynu Bükükler (Efekan 1985) 4
Bradbury-Rance, Clara 49
Braidotti, Rosi 17, 18, 42
Brogalin, Giovanni 4
Bulutları Beklerken / *Waiting for the Clouds* (Ustaoğlu 2003) 88
Burning (Changdong 2018) 11

Cannes 16, 21, 67, 70, 74, 84
Ceuterick, Maud 40, 42, 56
censorship 32, 94
Ceylan, Nuri Bilge 4, 9, 50, 63, 68, 89n1
child-stars 4, of Turkish cinema 5
Chion, Michel 35
chromo-politics, affirmative 63–5
cinematography 19, 30, 42, 44, 47, 51, 54, 72
colour 63–5
coming-of-age: absence/presence of willfulness 3–11; female coming-of-age 1, 2, 13, 68, 70, 80, 93; global trends of 11–13; narratives 2, 7, 19, 23, 43, 53; in Turkish cinema 51
Coppola, Sofia 41n3, 43, 63, 73
cross-cultural authorship *see* authorship

cross-cultural mobility 18, 93
Crying Boy, The 4
Çekmeköy Underground (Türkmen 2014) 6, 46, 53
Çiçekoğlu, Feride 40n2, 41n2
Çoğunluk / *Majority* (Yüce 2010) 6, 9, 46, 49, 51, 58, 59
Çöpçatan / *The Matchmaker* (İnanoğlu 1962) 3

Dadak, Zeynep 6, 43
Daha / *More* (Saylak 2017) 46, 53, 58, 63
Deleuze, Gilles 40
Demirkubuz, Zeki 33, 50
Denis, Claire 42, 84
#*DirenGezi* 19, 31, 60
Doane, Mary Ann 36
Driscoll, Catherine 12, 27
Drop of Water, A (Ergüven 2006) 14

Ece: suicide 28–30, 37, 48, 61; *see also* anti-feminist discourses; voice-off
Edge of Heaven, The (Akın 2007) 95
Elsaesser, Thomas 51, 74, 75
Erdem, Reha 6, 34, 43, 52, 63
Erdoğan, Recep Tayyip 13, 22, 25–9; anti-abortion 31; voice-off 31; *see also* anti-feminist discourses; New Turkey; politics of intimate; speaking state
Ergüven, Deniz Gamze 1, 2, 7, 15, 22, 23, 32, 44, 47, 49, 55, 56, 68, 76, 77, 82–4, 92
Eşkıya / *The Bandit* (Turgul 1996) 33
European cinema 2, 14, 44, 51

familialism 4, 11, 18, 25, 31, 34; familialist ideals 35; neoconservative 31
female agency 19, 34, 69, 72, 79, 92
female authorship *see* authorship
femicides 29, 31; *see also* transfemicide
feminism: affirmative 2; transnational 1, 15, 60, 92; Western 69, 88
feminists social movements 31
Ferah Feza / *Ships* (Refiğ 2013) 46, 53, 63
Fire (Mehta 1996) 16

five-headed 51, 58; creature 44–50

Gavron, Sarah 43
Geçen Yaz / *Last Summer* (Açıktan 2021) 53, 93
Gegen die Wand / *Head-On* (Akın 2004) 42, 91n15
Gelecek Uzun Sürer / *Future Lasts Forever* (Alper 2011) 7, 46, 52
Gemide / *On Board* (Akar 1998) 33
gender and sexuality, politics of 16, 18, 19, 25, 42
gender-based violence 6, 19, 22, 34; in AKP's 'New Turkey' 29; cinematic response to 36; depiction of 65; normalisation of 25; public protests and social media campaigns against 31; relation with sexist political statements 29
gender equality 25, 28, 39, 93
gender norms, 27, 29, 30, 52, 64
gender politics, of 'New Turkey' 3, 13, 17–18, 22, 25, 29, 31, 35–6, 51, 69, 92
Gezi Park protests 7, 19, 31–2
Gillibert, Charles 67, 84, 85
Giovanetti, Guillaume 43, 57
girlhood 13, 19, 47, 59, 66, 69, 71–2, 74, 85, 93; willful 66, 68, 73, 80, 82
Girlhood (Sciamma 2014) 11, 43, 47, 49, 50, 53
Gökçe, Övgü 52

Hababam Sınıfı / *The Chaos Class* (Eğilmez 1975) 4
Hadi İnşallah / *Hopefully* (Baltacı 2014) 9
Hayaletler / *Ghosts* (Okyay 2020) 34, 53, 93
Hayat Var / *My Only Sunshine* (Erdem 2008) 6, 7, 8, 34, 43, 46, 58, 63, 66n1
Hep Ezildim (Gürsu 1989) 4
Hollywood 7, 12, 51, 88

identity politics 48, 66
inter-generational conflicts 27, 34
interstitial 11, 16, 61, 68, 92, 95; aesthetics 44, authorship 6, 57; filmmaking 1, 17; interstitiality 15; location 2, 66; media 17

In the Fade (Akın 2019) 95
İnsanlar İkiye Ayrılır / *Two Types of People* (Şahin 2020) 93
İstanbul Convention 11
İşe Yarar Bir Şey / *Something Useful* (Esmer 2017) 34

Jîn (Erdem 2013) 34, 46, 52, 66n1
Johnston, Claire 87
joy 7, 10, 22, 24, 36–8, 40, 48–9, 55, 63
Justice and Development Party *see* AKP

Kağıttan Hayatlar / *Paper Lives* (Ulkay 2021) 93
Kandiyoti, Deniz 29, 30; *see also* masculinist restoration
Kara Köpekler Havlarken / *Black Dogs Barking* (Er and Gorbach 2009) 6, 46
Kar / *Snow* (Erdoğdu 2017) 6, 34, 46
Kayan, Merve 6, 43
Kaygı / *Inflame* (Özçelik 2017) 7, 46, 52
Kelebekler / *Butterflies* (Karaçelik 2018) 77
Kings (Ergüven 2017) 21n5, 76
Kış Uykusu / *Winter Sleep* (Ceylan 2015) 68
Kızkardeşler / *A Tale of Three Sisters* (Alper 2019) 7, 52
Koca Dünya / *Big Big World* (Erdem 2016) 6, 46, 49, 51
Kocan Kadar Konuş: Diriliş / *Husband Factor: Resurrection* (Baruönü 2016) 9
Kocan Kadar Konuş / *Husband Factor* (Baruönü 2015) 9
Köksüz / *Nobody's Home* (Akçay 2013) 34, 59
Korkman, Zeynep 27, 31
Kurtuluş: Son Durak / *Last Stop: Kurtulus* (Pirhasan 2012) 34
Kuzu / *The Lamb* (Ataman 2014) 52, 59

Labaki, Nadine 16, 73
La Fate Ignoranti (Özpetek 2001) 95
La Fémis 14, 82, 84, 91n14

Index

La Haine (1995) 53
Lale 9, 22, 24, 26, 30, 36, 39, 48–9, 54, 63–5; dream scenes 36–7; escape plan 38–9; point of view 35, 48, 71; voice-over 24, 35–6, 48, 50
Le Monde 67
LGBTQ+ 31, 93; as family-breakers 26; hate speech against 11; politics of intimate 31
Libération 67
Liberty Leading the People (1830) 60
liminality 12, 68
Love 101, 94

macho cinema 33
male: -centred narratives 18–19, 22, 32–3; characters 54; films 33; violence 30–1; weepy films 33
Marciniak, Katarzyna 75, 76, 79, 81–2, 86, 89, 91n13, 96; *see also* palatable foreignness
Martin, Adrian 12
masculinist restoration 30; *see also* Kandiyoti, Deniz
Masumiyet / Innocence (Demirkubuz 1997) 33
maternal: characters 58; closet 58–63
Mavi Dalga / The Blue Wave (Dadak and Kayan 2013) 6, 10, 34, 35, 43, 53
Mehta, Deepa 16, 85, 96
Messidor (Tanner 1979) 42
migrant 1, 13–18, 20n3, 68, 74, 88, 92, 95–6; 'migrant-by-choice' identity 68
mise-en-scène 10, 19, 44, 47, 50, 51, 54, 61, 63, 65
Mon trajet préféré (Ergüven 2006) 14
motherhood 22, 28, 58–9

Naficy, Hamid 14, 15, 68, 96
Naissance des Pieuvres / Water Lillies (Sciamma, 2007) 53, 62
Nar / Pomegranate (Ünal 2011) 34
national cinema 44, 66, 74, 77; in Turkey 77
national identity 20, 23, 39, 52, 91n12
Nefesim Kesilene Kadar / Until I Lose My Breath (Balcı 2015) 6, 34, 43, 46, 53, 63

Neşeli Günler / Happy Days (Aksoy 1978) 4
Neshat, Shirin 85, 96
New Cinema of Turkey 32, 37, 50, 58, 65
New Turkey 18, 22, 26–7; gender politics of 29, 35; 'pious generation' 39; 'wife factory' 23, 24–8
New Turkish Cinema *see* New Cinema of Turkey
new women's narratives 18, 32–3, 35, 92; *see also* New Cinema of Turkey
Nur 30, 62; sexual abuse 59

Öksüzler / Orphans (Göreç 1986) 4
Özpetek, Ferzan 84, 95–6

palatable foreignness 21n5, 65–6, 75, 76, 79, 86; *see also* Marciniak, Katarzyna
Pandoranın Kutusu / Pandora's Box (Ustaoğlu 2008) 68
Paradoxes of Political Art, The 40
Pariah (Rees 2011) 49–50
patriarchal: family 6, 9, 26; gender order 7; gender politics 57; governance 31; language 84; values 3, 7, 62; viewpoint 79
Persepolis (Satrapi 2007) 16
pious generation 39
poetic realism 48, 51, 52
politics of intimate 31
politics of location 16, 69, 79

queer adolescence 49–50
queer social movements 31

Rancière, Jacques 40
Regnier, Isabelle 67, 72
Rich, Adrienne 69
Rocks (2019) 43
Romantik Komedi: Bekarlığa Veda / Romantic Comedy: Stag Party (Özlevi 2013) 9
Romantik Komedi / Romantic Comedy (Ketche 2010) 9
Romantik / Romantic (Çetin 2007) 33

Sacred Heart (2005) 95
Sardunya / Geranium (Bocut 2021) 93

Scattered Hegemonies 69
Sciamma, Céline 43, 53, 62, 84; *Girlhood* (2014) 11, 43, 53; *Naissance des Pieuvres / Water Lillies* (2007) 53, 62; *Tomboy* (2011) 53
self-realisation 32, 34
Selma 30, 47–8, 61–2
sexuality 4, 16, 18–20, 25–6, 31, 42, 46, 51, 61, 63, 64, 70–2, 80
Sezercik Aslan Parçası (1972) 5
Sezercik Küçük Mücahit (Göreç 1974) 3
'shit-coloured' dresses 26, 30, 37, 39, 65
Sibel (Zencirci and Giovanetti 2018) 7, 34, 43, 57
Silverman, Kaja 35
Sivas (Müjdeci 2014) 9, 52
Sıfır Bir / Zero Zone (Taşkın 2020) 93
Smith, Frances 53, 62; *banlieue* 54
social realism 48, 51
Sofra Sırları / Serial Cook (Ünal 2017) 34, 35, 38
Sonay 30, 47, 54, 61, 62, 64
Sonbahar / Autumn (Alper 2008) 7, 46, 52
Soul Kitchen (Akın 2009) 95
Söylemez, Belmin 6, 43
spaces of flight 54, 55
speaking state 29, 31, 35, 36 *see also* Atuk, Sumru
Suner, Asuman 50, 77, 88, 90n9
Süt / Milk (Kaplanoğlu 2008) 59
Şimdiki Zaman / Present Tense (Söylemez 2012) 6, 10, 34–5, 43, 46, 49, 51, 52, 66n1

Tamam Mıyız? / Are We Okay? (Irmak 2013) 59
Tanner, Alain 42
taşra 50, 52, 57, 58, 77; allegorical affiliations of 53; rural landscapes 52; *taşra* films 17, 73
teen film 12, 27, 49; teen girl film 89
Tepenin Ardı / Beyond the Hills (2012) 46, 52
Tereddüt / Clair-Obscur (Ustaoğlu 2016) 7, 34, 35, 38
Tomboy (Sciamma, 2011) 53

Toz Bezi / Dust Cloth (Öztürk 2015) 34
transfemicide 31; *see also* femicides
transnational 87–8; affinities 75–82, cinema 14, 44, 74; female authorship 82; feminist world cinema 81; film 42, 68, 83; filmmaking 2, 3, 13, 66, 82
Transnational Feminism in Film and Media (2007) 96
Turkish cinema 33, 49, 50, 52, 58, 60, 63, 70, 90n9; *see also* New Cinema of Turkey

Uzak / Distant (Ceylan 2002) 33
Üç Maymun / Three Monkeys (Ceylan 2008) 9, 46, 58, 59, 63

Vendredi Soir / Friday Night (2002) 42
Virgin Suicides, The (1999) 41n3, 43, 63, 76
voice: voice-off 22, 29, 31; voice-over 9, 24, 35–6, 41n3, 48–50, 71; female voice 19, 22–3; *see also* Lale
Voice in Cinema, The 35, 36

Wadjda (2012) 42, 56
White, Patricia 76, 85
'wife-factory' 9, 23, 24–8, 30, 34, 39; house-as-'wife factory' 28; of Turkish political context 26
willful 6, 42, 44; youth 18, 42; *see also* girlhood
willfulness 3–11, 12, 18, 22, 37, 41n4, 43, 47, 58–9, 63, 70
Willful Subjects (2014) 5, 37, 42
Wilson, Emma 62
Winocour, Alice 21n5, 84
womanhood: 'proper' 7, 9, 27, 28–32, 38; AKP's familialist ideals of 35
women directors 34, 41n4, 58, 85
women's agency 18, 34
women's cinema 15, 32–6, 76–7, 79, 87; *see also* women's filmmaking
Women's Cinema as Counter-Cinema (1973) 87
Women's Cinema, World Cinema (2015) 15, 96
women's filmmaking 2, 15; aesthetics 75; world cinemas 2

women's rights 18, 25, 30, 74
World Cinema 1–2, 13–15, 17, 44, 48, 63, 66, 74–7, 81, 87–9, 90n8, 92, 96
Wyatt, Justin 63

Xiaolu Guo 85

Yatçi, Delal 41n4
Yeniden Leyla / Leyla, Once Again (Hancıoğulları 2020) 93
Yeşilçam 3, 5, 6, 58, 59
youth: female youth 23; youth femininities 1; 'proper' 32; representation 2
youth films: current trends of 44; global youth films 11, 17; post-millennial 52; in Turkish cinema 6, 36
Yumurcak Belalı Tatil / The Man from Chicago (Koloğlu, Melikyan, and Pallardy 1975) 3
Yumurcak (İnanoğlu 1969) 3
Yumurcak Köprü Altı Çocuğu (İnanoğlu 1970) 3
Yuvasızlar (1987) 5

Zavallılar / The Poor Ones (Efekan 1984) 4
Zefir (Baş 2010) 34, 52, 59
Zencirci, Çağla 7, 43, 57
Zenne / The Dancer (Alper and Binay 2011) 6, 59

Printed in the United States
by Baker & Taylor Publisher Services